KIM MIA

LAKE TAHOE
TRAVEL GUIDE
2025

Your Ultimate Guidebook to Breathtaking Scenery, Outdoor Adventures, Top Resorts, and Hidden Gems in America's Alpine Paradise.

SCAN THIS QR CODE FOR PICTURES AND MAP

CONTENTS

CHAPTER 1: WELCOME TO LAKE TAHOE
1.1 INTRODUCTION TO LAKE TAHOE: A YEAR-ROUND PARADISE

Nestled in the Sierra Nevada mountains, Lake Tahoe is a stunning gem that straddles the border between California and Nevada. Renowned for its crystal-clear waters and breathtaking alpine scenery, Lake Tahoe offers a unique blend of natural beauty, outdoor adventures, and vibrant local culture. Whether you're drawn to its shimmering blue waters in the summer or the powdery slopes in the winter, Lake Tahoe is a year-round paradise that attracts visitors from all walks of life.

Lake Tahoe's history is as rich as its landscape. Formed over two million years ago during the ice ages, this pristine lake has been a gathering place for humans for thousands of years. Native American tribes, including the Washoe people, first inhabited the region, relying on the lake for sustenance and spiritual connection. The discovery of gold and silver in the mid-19th century brought a wave of settlers and prospectors to the area, and Lake Tahoe quickly became a sought-after destination.

In the late 19th and early 20th centuries, Lake Tahoe gained popularity as a summer retreat for the wealthy. Grand lodges and luxurious estates were built along its shores, drawing celebrities and dignitaries from across the country. Today, while much has changed, Lake Tahoe still retains its allure as a premier destination, blending its historical charm with modern amenities.

One of the most remarkable aspects of Lake Tahoe is its ability to transform with the seasons, offering a distinct experience no matter the time of year.

- **Winter Wonderland:** Lake Tahoe is world-famous for its winter sports, particularly skiing and snowboarding. The region boasts several renowned ski resorts, including Heavenly, Squaw Valley, and Northstar, each offering a unique mix of terrain, from challenging black diamonds to gentle beginner slopes. Snowshoeing, cross-country skiing, and ice skating are also popular activities, and the après-ski scene is vibrant, with cozy lodges and fine dining options.

- **Spring Awakening:** As the snow begins to melt, Lake Tahoe undergoes a stunning transformation. The spring months bring a burst of wildflowers, and the hiking trails, once blanketed in snow, become accessible again. This is the perfect time to explore the lush forests, cascading waterfalls, and panoramic vistas that surround the lake. Spring is also a quieter season, offering a peaceful retreat before the summer crowds arrive.

- **Summer Escape:** Summer at Lake Tahoe is nothing short of magical. The lake's clear, turquoise waters invite visitors to swim, kayak, paddleboard, and sail. Beaches such as Sand Harbor and Zephyr Cove are popular spots for sunbathing and picnicking. Hiking, mountain biking, and rock climbing are also in full swing, with trails that range from leisurely strolls to challenging ascents. For those who enjoy fishing, Lake Tahoe is home to a variety of species, including trout and salmon. The summer months also bring a host of festivals, outdoor concerts, and events, adding a lively atmosphere to the serene surroundings.

- **Autumn Serenity:** Fall in Lake Tahoe is a time of tranquility and reflection. The aspen trees turn golden, and the air is crisp and cool. It's an ideal season for scenic drives, particularly along the Lake Tahoe Scenic Byway, where you can take in the vibrant fall foliage. Hiking and biking trails are less crowded, and the lake itself remains a stunning backdrop for relaxation and outdoor exploration. Autumn is also the perfect time to visit local wineries and enjoy farm-to-table dining experiences that showcase the region's harvest.

Lake Tahoe's outdoor attractions are as diverse as its seasons. In addition to the myriad of seasonal activities, the area is home to several must-see natural wonders and landmarks.

- **Emerald Bay State Park:** Known for its striking emerald-green waters, this state park is one of Lake Tahoe's most photographed locations. Visitors can explore the historic Vikingsholm mansion, hike the Rubicon Trail, or take a boat tour to Fannette Island, the only island in Lake Tahoe.

- **Heavenly Mountain Resort:** Offering breathtaking views of the lake and surrounding mountains, Heavenly is a year-round destination. In winter, it's a premier ski resort, and in summer, visitors can take a scenic gondola ride to the top of the mountain for panoramic views and access to hiking trails.

- **Desolation Wilderness:** For those seeking solitude and adventure, Desolation Wilderness is a pristine area offering rugged terrain, alpine lakes, and towering peaks. It's a popular destination for backpacking, with numerous trails that lead to remote campsites and hidden gems.

- **Lake Tahoe Nevada State Park:** This park offers a variety of recreational activities, including hiking, picnicking, and wildlife viewing. Sand Harbor, within the park, is a popular spot for beachgoers and a venue for the annual Lake Tahoe Shakespeare Festival.

- **Truckee River:** Flowing out of Lake Tahoe, the Truckee River is a hub for water sports such as rafting and tubing. The river also offers excellent fishing opportunities and scenic spots for picnics.

Beyond its natural beauty, Lake Tahoe has a vibrant local culture that is deeply connected to the outdoors. The towns surrounding the lake, such as South Lake Tahoe, Tahoe City, and Incline Village, offer a charming blend of rustic mountain vibes and modern amenities. Art galleries, boutique shops, and local markets showcase the talents and crafts of the region's artisans.

The community is also committed to preserving the environment and promoting sustainable tourism. Numerous initiatives are in place to protect the lake's clarity and the surrounding wilderness areas, ensuring that future generations can continue to enjoy this remarkable destination.

Whether you're an adrenaline junkie, a nature lover, or someone simply seeking a peaceful escape, Lake Tahoe has something to offer. Its year-round appeal lies in its ability to cater to a wide range of interests and activities. From the thrill of carving through fresh powder on a winter's day to the serenity of watching the sunset over the lake in summer, Lake Tahoe is a place where memories are made.

In Lake Tahoe, every visit is a new adventure, and every season brings a different kind of magic. As you explore its shores, mountains, and forests, you'll quickly understand why this destination has captivated visitors for generations and continues to be a beloved retreat for all who experience its beauty.

1.2 HOW TO GET THERE

Visiting Lake Tahoe is an unforgettable experience, and getting there is a journey filled with excitement and anticipation. Whether you're flying in from afar or driving from a nearby city, this guide will help you navigate the logistics of getting to Lake Tahoe, including flight options, ticket booking, visa requirements, and transportation to and from the airport.

1. FLYING TO LAKE TAHOE

The closest major airports to Lake Tahoe are Reno-Tahoe International Airport (RNO) in Nevada and Sacramento International Airport (SMF) in California. Both airports offer convenient access to the region, with various airlines providing direct flights from major U.S. cities.

- **Reno-Tahoe International Airport (RNO):** Located approximately 60 miles (97 kilometers) from Lake Tahoe, this airport is the most popular choice for travelers heading to the lake. It's well-connected with daily flights from cities like Los Angeles, San Francisco, Denver, and Chicago.

- **Sacramento International Airport (SMF):** Situated about 120 miles (193 kilometers) from Lake Tahoe, Sacramento International

Airport serves as another gateway to the region. It offers numerous flights from major U.S. hubs, making it a viable option for travelers.

For those traveling internationally, the closest airports with international flights are San Francisco International Airport (SFO) and Los Angeles International Airport (LAX), both of which offer a wide range of connecting flights to Reno or Sacramento.

2. BOOKING FLIGHTS AND TICKETS

Booking your flight to Lake Tahoe is straightforward, with numerous online platforms offering competitive prices and various travel options. Here are some recommended websites for booking flights:

- **Expedia:** www.expedia.com
  Offers a comprehensive search engine that allows you to compare flight prices, book accommodations, and rent cars all in one place.

- **Google Flights:** www.google.com/flights
  A user-friendly tool that lets you track prices and find the best deals on flights.

- **Kayak:** www.kayak.com
  Another great platform to compare flights from different airlines and set up price alerts.

- **Skyscanner:** www.skyscanner.com
  Known for finding budget-friendly options, Skyscanner is ideal for those looking for the best deals.

- **Airline Websites:** You can also book directly through airline websites, such as Delta, United, Southwest, and others, to manage your bookings and explore flight options.

3. VISA REQUIREMENTS

If you are traveling from outside the United States, it's essential to check the visa requirements before planning your trip to Lake Tahoe.

- **Visa Waiver Program (VWP):** Citizens of certain countries can travel to the U.S. for tourism or business purposes for up to 90 days without a visa under the Visa Waiver Program. However, you must apply for authorization through the Electronic System for Travel Authorization (ESTA) before traveling. Visit the official ESTA website to apply.

- **Tourist Visa (B-2):** Travelers not eligible for the VWP will need to apply for a B-2 tourist visa. The application process involves filling out the DS-160 form, paying the visa fee, and scheduling an interview at your nearest U.S. embassy or consulate. Visit the U.S. Department of State's official website for more information.

4. GETTING TO THE AIRPORT

Depending on where you're flying from, getting to your departure airport can be simple or require a bit of planning. Here are some tips to ensure a smooth journey:

- **Public Transportation:** Many major cities offer public transportation options like buses, trains, and subways that connect directly to the airport. This is often the most cost-effective way to reach the airport.

- **Airport Shuttles:** Various shuttle services operate in cities across the U.S., providing convenient, door-to-door transportation to the airport. Companies like SuperShuttle, Go Airport Shuttle, and local services often provide reliable options.

- **Ride-Sharing Services:** Services like Uber and Lyft offer convenient and flexible transportation to the airport. You can schedule a ride in advance or request one on-demand using their apps.

- **Driving and Parking:** If you prefer to drive yourself, most airports offer short-term and long-term parking options. Booking your parking spot in advance through platforms like SpotHero can save you time and money.

5. LEAVING THE AIRPORT AND REACHING LAKE TAHOE

Upon arrival at either Reno-Tahoe International Airport or Sacramento International Airport, you have several options to reach Lake Tahoe.

- **Car Rentals:** Renting a car is one of the most convenient ways to explore Lake Tahoe and its surroundings. Both RNO and SMF airports host major car rental agencies such as Hertz, Avis, Enterprise, and Budget. Renting a car allows you the flexibility to travel at your own pace and explore the scenic routes to Lake Tahoe.

- **Airport Shuttles:** Several shuttle services operate between the airports and Lake Tahoe. Companies like South Tahoe Airporter provide scheduled services from Reno-Tahoe International Airport to South Lake Tahoe. Shuttle services can be pre-booked online or upon arrival at the airport.

- **Private Transfers:** For a more comfortable and personalized experience, private transfer services are available. Companies like Black Tie Transportation offer luxury vehicles and door-to-door service, ensuring a smooth and hassle-free journey to your destination.

- **Ride-Sharing Services:** Uber and Lyft operate in both Reno and Sacramento, providing a convenient way to reach Lake Tahoe. These services are readily available at the airports, and you can request a ride directly through their apps.

- **Public Transportation:** If you're looking for a budget-friendly option, public transportation is available from both airports to Lake Tahoe. From Reno-Tahoe International Airport, you can take the RTC Ride bus to the Reno Greyhound Station and then a Greyhound bus to South Lake Tahoe. From Sacramento, you can take a shuttle to the Sacramento Amtrak station and then a train to Truckee, followed by a local bus to Tahoe.

1.3 Essential Travel Tips

Traveling to Lake Tahoe is an exciting experience, filled with the promise of adventure, relaxation, and stunning natural beauty. To ensure your trip goes smoothly, here are some essential travel tips that will help you make the most of your visit, no matter the season.

1. Check the Weather

Lake Tahoe's weather can be unpredictable, especially in the mountains, where conditions can change rapidly. Before you pack your bags, check the weather forecast to ensure you're prepared for whatever Mother Nature has in store.

- **Winter:** If you're visiting in winter, expect cold temperatures and possibly heavy snowfall. Be sure to pack warm, waterproof clothing, including a good quality winter coat, gloves, and thermal layers. Snow boots with good traction are also essential.

- **Summer:** In summer, the days can be warm and sunny, but evenings can still be cool, especially at higher elevations. Bring a mix of lightweight, breathable clothing for daytime activities and warmer layers for the evenings. Sunscreen, sunglasses, and a hat are also must-haves to protect against the strong sun.

- **Spring and Fall:** These shoulder seasons can bring a mix of weather, from sunny days to unexpected rain showers or even snow. Dress in layers, and be prepared for a variety of conditions.

2. Altitude Awareness

Lake Tahoe sits at an elevation of about 6,225 feet (1,897 meters) above sea level, and many of the surrounding mountains reach even higher. If you're not accustomed to higher altitudes, you might experience symptoms of altitude sickness, such as headaches, dizziness, or shortness of breath.

- **Stay Hydrated:** Drink plenty of water to help your body adjust to the altitude.

- **Take it Slow:** Give yourself time to acclimate, especially on your first day. Avoid strenuous activities until you've had a chance to get used to the elevation.

- **Be Aware of Symptoms:** If you experience severe symptoms like shortness of breath, nausea, or extreme fatigue, it's important to descend to a lower altitude and seek medical attention if needed.

3. BOOK ACCOMMODATION IN ADVANCE

Lake Tahoe is a popular destination year-round, and accommodations can fill up quickly, especially during peak seasons like summer and winter holidays. To secure the best options, it's wise to book your lodging well in advance.

- **Peak Seasons:** During ski season (December to March) and summer (June to August), hotels, cabins, and vacation rentals can be in high demand. Booking early not only ensures availability but also gives you access to better rates.

- **Off-Peak Seasons:** If you're visiting during the quieter months of spring or fall, you may find more availability and better deals, but it's still a good idea to book in advance, particularly if you have specific preferences.

4. PLAN YOUR TRANSPORTATION

While Lake Tahoe is accessible by car, navigating the area can be challenging, especially in winter when snow and ice can make driving conditions difficult. Consider these transportation tips:

- **Renting a Car:** If you plan to explore different parts of Lake Tahoe, renting a car is the most convenient option. Ensure your rental car is equipped with snow tires or chains during the winter months.

- **Public Transportation:** Lake Tahoe has a limited public transportation system, but it can be a good option if you're staying in a well-connected area. The Tahoe Transportation District operates buses that run between key locations around the lake.

- **Parking:** During peak seasons, parking at popular trailheads, beaches, and ski resorts can be limited. Arrive early to secure a spot, or consider using shuttles or ride-sharing services.

5. STAY SAFE ON THE TRAILS AND SLOPES

Whether you're hiking, skiing, or snowboarding, safety should always be your top priority.

- **Know Your Limits:** Lake Tahoe's trails and slopes offer challenges for all skill levels, but it's important to choose routes and activities that match your abilities. Don't push yourself beyond your comfort zone, especially in remote areas.

- **Bring the Essentials:** Always carry a map, compass, or GPS device, and make sure your phone is fully charged before heading out. Pack a first-aid kit, snacks, and plenty of water, especially on longer hikes.

- **Respect the Environment:** Lake Tahoe is a pristine natural area, and it's important to leave no trace. Stay on marked trails, dispose of trash properly, and avoid disturbing wildlife.

6. PREPARE FOR EMERGENCIES

While Lake Tahoe is a well-developed area, it's still a mountain environment where weather and conditions can change quickly. Be prepared for emergencies by following these tips:

- **Emergency Contacts:** Familiarize yourself with the local emergency numbers, and know the location of the nearest hospital or urgent care facility.

- **Weather Alerts:** Sign up for local weather alerts on your phone to stay informed about any sudden changes in conditions.

- **Emergency Kit:** If you're driving, keep an emergency kit in your car that includes blankets, a flashlight, non-perishable food, and a snow shovel in winter.

7. RESPECT LOCAL WILDLIFE

Lake Tahoe is home to a variety of wildlife, including bears, coyotes, and mountain lions. While encounters are rare, it's important to respect their habitat and follow safety guidelines.

- **Bear Safety:** If you're camping or hiking, store food in bear-proof containers and never leave food unattended. If you encounter a bear, make yourself look large, make noise, and slowly back away. Never run.

- **Leave No Trace:** Wildlife can be easily disturbed by human activity. Stick to marked trails, avoid feeding animals, and keep your distance when observing wildlife.

8. EXPLORE OFF THE BEATEN PATH

While Lake Tahoe's popular spots are well worth visiting, don't be afraid to explore some of the lesser-known areas for a more peaceful experience.

- **Hidden Beaches:** Lake Tahoe is dotted with smaller, more secluded beaches that offer a tranquil alternative to the busier spots. Secret Cove and Hidden Beach are two great options.

- **Backcountry Adventures:** For those looking to escape the crowds, the backcountry around Lake Tahoe offers incredible opportunities for hiking, skiing, and camping. Just be sure you're prepared and experienced enough for the challenges of the wilderness.

- **Local Culture:** Explore the small towns around Lake Tahoe to get a taste of local life. Visit local markets, art galleries, and historical sites to connect with the area's rich culture and history.

9. STAY CONNECTED

While Lake Tahoe offers a great escape from the hustle and bustle, staying connected is still important, especially if you're in remote areas.

- **Cell Service:** Cell service can be spotty in some parts of Lake Tahoe, particularly in the mountains and wilderness areas. Be prepared for limited coverage and plan accordingly.

- **Wi-Fi Access:** Most hotels, resorts, and cafes in Lake Tahoe offer Wi-Fi access. If you need a reliable connection, consider bringing a mobile hotspot or checking in advance if your accommodation offers high-speed internet.

- **Emergency Communication:** In areas with no cell service, consider carrying a satellite phone or a personal locator beacon (PLB) for emergencies.

10. ENJOY THE LOCAL CUISINE

No trip to Lake Tahoe is complete without sampling the local food scene. From gourmet dining to casual eateries, the area offers a wide range of culinary delights.

- **Farm-to-Table:** Many restaurants in Lake Tahoe pride themselves on using fresh, local ingredients. Try a farm-to-table restaurant for a true taste of the region.

- **Seafood:** Despite being in the mountains, Lake Tahoe offers excellent seafood options, with fresh fish often flown in daily.

- **Local Favorites:** Don't miss out on trying local favorites like Tahoe-style pizza, hearty mountain breakfasts, and craft beers from local breweries.

1.4 FAQs for First-Time Visitors

1. What is the best time of year to visit Lake Tahoe?

Answer: Lake Tahoe is a year-round destination, offering unique experiences in every season.

- **Winter (December to March):** Ideal for skiing, snowboarding, and other winter sports. The mountains are covered in snow, and the ski resorts are in full swing.

- **Spring (April to June):** A quieter time with fewer crowds. The snow begins to melt, making way for wildflowers and accessible hiking trails.

- **Summer (July to September):** Perfect for water activities, hiking, and enjoying the warm weather. This is the busiest season, so expect more tourists.

- **Fall (October to November):** A great time for scenic drives, hiking, and enjoying the fall foliage. The weather is cooler, and the area is less crowded.

2. How do I get to Lake Tahoe?

Answer: Lake Tahoe can be reached by car, plane, or public transportation.

- **By Air:** The closest major airports are Reno-Tahoe International Airport (RNO) and Sacramento International Airport (SMF). From these airports, you can rent a car, take a shuttle, or use ride-sharing services to reach Lake Tahoe.

- **By Car:** If you're driving, Lake Tahoe is accessible via major highways, including I-80 and US-50.

- **Public Transportation:** Buses and shuttles are available from nearby cities, including Reno and Sacramento.

3. DO I NEED A CAR WHILE VISITING LAKE TAHOE?

Answer: While having a car is convenient, especially if you plan to explore different parts of the lake, it's not strictly necessary.

- **Public Transportation:** The Tahoe Transportation District operates buses around the lake, connecting major towns and attractions.

- **Shuttles and Ride-Sharing:** Many resorts offer shuttle services, and ride-sharing apps like Uber and Lyft are available.

- **Biking and Walking:** Depending on where you stay, biking and walking can be great ways to explore the area.

4. WHAT SHOULD I PACK FOR MY TRIP TO LAKE TAHOE?

Answer: What you pack depends on the season of your visit.

- **Winter:** Warm, waterproof clothing, snow boots, gloves, hats, and scarves. Don't forget sunglasses, as the sun reflecting off the snow can be intense.

- **Summer:** Lightweight, breathable clothing, a hat, sunglasses, sunscreen, and comfortable hiking shoes. Pack layers for cooler evenings.

- **Spring/Fall:** A mix of warm and cool clothing, including layers. Waterproof gear is also a good idea in case of rain.

- **Year-Round Essentials:** Always pack a good pair of hiking shoes, a reusable water bottle, and a camera to capture the stunning scenery.

5. ARE THERE ANY ENTRY FEES FOR VISITING LAKE TAHOE?

Answer: Lake Tahoe itself is free to visit, but some specific areas and activities may require fees.

- **State Parks:** Many of Lake Tahoe's state parks, like Emerald Bay State Park, charge a day-use fee. The fee typically ranges from $5 to $10 per vehicle.

- **Parking:** Some popular beaches and trailheads may charge for parking.

- **Recreation Activities:** Ski resorts, boat rentals, and other recreational activities have their own fees.

6. WHAT ARE THE BEST ACTIVITIES TO DO IN LAKE TAHOE?

Answer: Lake Tahoe offers a wide range of activities depending on the season.

- **Winter:** Skiing, snowboarding, snowshoeing, ice skating, and snowmobiling.

- **Summer:** Swimming, kayaking, paddleboarding, hiking, biking, and boating.

- **Spring/Fall:** Hiking, scenic drives, fishing, and enjoying the local culture and cuisine.

- **Year-Round:** Exploring the local towns, visiting art galleries, dining at local restaurants, and relaxing by the lake.

7. IS LAKE TAHOE FAMILY-FRIENDLY?

Answer: Absolutely! Lake Tahoe is a fantastic destination for families, offering a variety of activities suitable for all ages.

- **Family-Friendly Ski Resorts:** Many ski resorts offer lessons and activities for children.

- **Beaches:** The lake's beaches are perfect for swimming, picnicking, and building sandcastles.

- **Hiking Trails:** There are numerous easy-to-moderate hiking trails that are suitable for children and offer stunning views.

- **Events and Festivals:** Throughout the year, Lake Tahoe hosts family-friendly events, including outdoor concerts, festivals, and holiday celebrations.

8. ARE PETS ALLOWED AT LAKE TAHOE?

Answer: Yes, Lake Tahoe is pet-friendly, but there are some guidelines to follow.

- **Leash Laws:** Dogs must be on a leash in most public areas, including state parks and beaches.

- **Pet-Friendly Accommodations:** Many hotels, cabins, and vacation rentals in Lake Tahoe welcome pets. It's always best to check the specific pet policy before booking.

- **Pet-Friendly Activities:** There are several pet-friendly trails and beaches, such as Kiva Beach on the south shore.

9. WHAT IS THE BEST WAY TO EXPLORE THE LAKE?

Answer: Exploring Lake Tahoe can be done in several exciting ways.

- **Driving:** A scenic drive around the lake on the Tahoe Rim Drive offers breathtaking views and access to various points of interest.

- **Boating:** Renting a boat or taking a guided boat tour is a great way to experience the lake from the water.

- **Hiking:** Numerous trails around the lake provide access to secluded spots and panoramic views.

- **Cycling:** The Tahoe East Shore Trail is a popular cycling route that offers stunning views of the lake.

10. WHAT ARE SOME MUST-SEE ATTRACTIONS AT LAKE TAHOE?

Answer:

- **Emerald Bay:** Known for its stunning views and the historic Vikingsholm mansion, Emerald Bay is a must-visit.

- **Sand Harbor:** A beautiful beach on the Nevada side, perfect for swimming and picnicking.

- **Heavenly Mountain Resort:** Offers year-round activities, including skiing in the winter and hiking and scenic gondola rides in the summer.

- **Desolation Wilderness:** A pristine wilderness area ideal for hiking and backpacking.

- **Truckee River:** Perfect for rafting, fishing, and scenic walks.

CHAPTER 2: LAKE TAHOE AT A GLANCE
2.1 OVERVIEW OF THE REGION

Lake Tahoe is a magnificent natural wonder, nestled in the Sierra Nevada mountains and straddling the border between California and Nevada. Known for its crystal-clear waters, striking alpine scenery, and a diverse array of activities, Lake Tahoe has long been a favorite destination for nature lovers, adventure seekers, and those simply looking to unwind in a serene environment. Here's an overview of this captivating region.

GEOGRAPHY AND LANDSCAPE

Lake Tahoe is the largest alpine lake in North America and the second deepest lake in the United States, with a depth of 1,645 feet (501 meters). The lake covers a surface area of about 191 square miles (495 square kilometers) and is surrounded by towering peaks that rise up to 10,000 feet (3,048 meters) above sea level.

The lake is split into two main regions: the North Shore and the South Shore, each offering a unique experience. The North Shore is known for its quieter, more relaxed atmosphere, while the South Shore is bustling with activity, offering a variety of entertainment options, including casinos, restaurants, and nightlife.

THE NORTH SHORE

The North Shore of Lake Tahoe, located primarily in California, is characterized by its charming, laid-back vibe. It's an area where you can find quiet beaches, serene hiking trails, and quaint mountain towns. Key destinations on the North Shore include:

- **Tahoe City:** A picturesque town that serves as a gateway to the North Shore. Tahoe City offers stunning lake views, charming shops, and a variety of dining options. It's also home to the Tahoe Maritime Museum and the Gatekeeper's Museum.

- **Kings Beach:** Known for its wide, sandy beach, Kings Beach is a popular spot for swimming, kayaking, and paddleboarding. The town also hosts a range of local events and festivals throughout the year.

- **Incline Village:** Located on the Nevada side of the North Shore, Incline Village is an upscale community known for its luxury resorts, golf courses, and private beaches. It's also home to the popular Diamond Peak Ski Resort.

THE SOUTH SHORE

The South Shore, located on the California-Nevada border, is the livelier side of Lake Tahoe. It's where you'll find a blend of outdoor adventure, entertainment, and nightlife. Key destinations on the South Shore include:

- **South Lake Tahoe:** The largest town on the lake, South Lake Tahoe is a bustling hub of activity. It offers a wide range of accommodations, from luxury resorts to cozy cabins, and is known for its vibrant dining and nightlife scene. The town also provides easy access to Heavenly Mountain Resort, one of the most popular ski destinations in the area.

- **Stateline:** Just across the Nevada border from South Lake Tahoe, Stateline is famous for its casinos and entertainment venues. It's a great spot for those looking to try their luck at the tables or catch a live show.

- **Emerald Bay:** One of the most photographed spots in Lake Tahoe, Emerald Bay is known for its stunning beauty, with emerald-green waters and the historic Vikingsholm mansion. It's a must-visit for anyone exploring the South Shore.

OUTDOOR RECREATION

Lake Tahoe is a year-round playground for outdoor enthusiasts, offering a wide range of activities across its diverse landscape. Whether you're visiting in the winter, summer, or somewhere in between, there's always something to do.

- **Winter Sports:** Lake Tahoe is a premier destination for winter sports, with several world-class ski resorts offering everything from downhill skiing and snowboarding to cross-country skiing and snowshoeing. Popular resorts include Heavenly, Squaw Valley, Northstar, and Kirkwood.

- **Summer Activities:** In the summer, the lake's clear waters and surrounding mountains become a haven for water sports, hiking, biking, and camping. Popular summer activities include boating, kayaking, paddleboarding, and swimming. The region also boasts hundreds of miles of hiking and biking trails, ranging from easy walks to challenging backcountry routes.

- **Year-Round Attractions:** Beyond the seasonal activities, Lake Tahoe offers a variety of year-round attractions. Visitors can explore the region's history at local museums, enjoy scenic drives along the lake, or take in breathtaking views from one of the many lookout points. The Lake Tahoe Scenic Byway, a 72-mile drive around the lake, is a must for anyone wanting to experience the region's beauty.

CULTURAL AND HISTORICAL SIGNIFICANCE

Lake Tahoe's rich cultural and historical heritage adds another layer of depth to the region. The lake was originally inhabited by the Washoe people, who revered it as a sacred place. European settlers arrived in the mid-19th century, attracted by the discovery of gold and silver, and the area quickly became a popular summer retreat for the wealthy.

- **Historical Sites:** Visitors can explore the region's history at sites like the Tallac Historic Site, which features restored estates from the early 20th century, and the Vikingsholm mansion, a historic home that's considered one of the finest examples of Scandinavian architecture in the United States.

- **Local Culture:** Lake Tahoe is also home to a vibrant arts and culture scene. Throughout the year, the region hosts a variety of festivals, concerts, and events, celebrating everything from local art to food and wine. The Lake Tahoe Shakespeare Festival, held at Sand Harbor, is a highlight of the summer season.

ENVIRONMENTAL STEWARDSHIP

Lake Tahoe's natural beauty is matched by the efforts to preserve and protect it. The region is committed to sustainable tourism and environmental stewardship, with numerous initiatives in place to maintain the lake's clarity and protect its surrounding wilderness areas.

- **Conservation Efforts:** Organizations like the Tahoe Regional Planning Agency (TRPA) and the League to Save Lake Tahoe are dedicated to preserving the lake's environment. Visitors are encouraged to follow Leave No Trace principles, respect wildlife, and participate in local conservation efforts.

- **Sustainable Tourism:** Many local businesses and attractions are committed to sustainability, offering eco-friendly accommodations, tours, and activities. From supporting local farmers to reducing plastic waste, the region's commitment to sustainability is evident in every aspect of its tourism industry.

GETTING AROUND LAKE TAHOE

Navigating Lake Tahoe is easy, with several options available for getting around the region.

- **Driving:** Renting a car is the most convenient way to explore the area, especially if you plan to visit multiple towns or trailheads. The roads around Lake Tahoe are well-maintained, but be prepared for winter driving conditions if you're visiting during the colder months.

- **Public Transportation:** The Tahoe Transportation District operates buses that connect the major towns and attractions around the lake. This is a great option for those who prefer not to drive.

- **Cycling and Walking:** Many areas around Lake Tahoe are pedestrian and cyclist-friendly, with dedicated paths and trails. This is an excellent way to explore the scenic beauty of the region at a leisurely pace.

2.2 HISTORY AND CULTURAL SIGNIFICANCE

Lake Tahoe's history is as rich and deep as its crystal-clear waters, weaving together the stories of Native American tribes, European settlers, and modern-day adventurers. The cultural significance of this region is evident in its historical landmarks, traditions, and the enduring respect for the natural environment that continues to shape the way of life around the lake. Here's a closer look at the history and cultural importance of Lake Tahoe.

THE WASHOE PEOPLE: FIRST INHABITANTS

Long before European settlers arrived, the Washoe people were the original inhabitants of the Lake Tahoe Basin. For thousands of years, they lived in harmony with the land, considering the lake a sacred place, which they called "Da ow a ga," meaning "edge of the lake."

- **Spiritual Connection:** The Washoe believed that Lake Tahoe was a gift from the Great Spirit, providing them with food, water, and shelter. They lived a nomadic lifestyle, moving between the lake and the surrounding mountains depending on the season. Fishing, hunting, and gathering were central to their way of life.

- **Cultural Practices:** The Washoe people held annual gatherings at Lake Tahoe, where they celebrated with ceremonies, dances, and communal meals. These gatherings reinforced their cultural ties and ensured the transmission of traditions from one generation to the next.

- **Preservation of Heritage:** Today, the Washoe Tribe continues to play an active role in preserving the cultural heritage of Lake Tahoe. They work with local organizations to protect sacred sites and educate visitors about the region's indigenous history.

EUROPEAN EXPLORATION AND THE GOLD RUSH

The first recorded sighting of Lake Tahoe by European settlers was in 1844, when explorer John C. Frémont and his guide, Kit Carson, encountered the lake during their westward expedition. The discovery of gold in California in 1848, followed by the Comstock Lode silver strike in Nevada in 1859, brought a wave of settlers, miners, and entrepreneurs to the region.

- **The Comstock Lode:** The discovery of silver in the nearby Virginia City led to a mining boom that significantly impacted Lake Tahoe.

The demand for timber to support the mining industry led to widespread logging in the Tahoe Basin, altering the landscape and affecting the local environment.

- **Development of Transportation:** To support the mining industry, new transportation routes were developed, including the construction of wagon roads and, later, railroads. These routes not only facilitated the movement of goods but also made Lake Tahoe more accessible to settlers and visitors.

- **First Resorts:** As the mining boom waned, attention turned to Lake Tahoe's natural beauty. In the late 19th century, the region began to develop as a tourist destination. Wealthy families from San Francisco and other cities built grand estates along the lake's shores, and the first resorts were established, offering visitors a chance to escape the hustle and bustle of city life.

THE RISE OF TOURISM: 20TH CENTURY TO PRESENT

The early 20th century marked a new era for Lake Tahoe, as it transitioned from a remote wilderness to a popular vacation destination. The advent of the automobile and the construction of highways made the lake more accessible to the general public.

- **Luxury Resorts:** The 1920s and 1930s saw the rise of luxury resorts catering to an elite clientele. Places like the Tahoe Tavern and Brockway Springs Hotel offered guests lavish accommodations, gourmet dining, and a range of outdoor activities, from boating to horseback riding.

- **Winter Sports:** The development of ski resorts in the 1930s and 1940s transformed Lake Tahoe into a year-round destination. The opening of the Squaw Valley Ski Resort and the subsequent hosting of the 1960 Winter Olympics put Lake Tahoe on the map as a premier destination for winter sports enthusiasts.

- **The Casino Boom:** The legalization of gambling in Nevada in 1931 led to the development of casinos on the Nevada side of Lake

Tahoe. Towns like Stateline and Crystal Bay became entertainment hubs, attracting visitors with their combination of gaming, live shows, and nightlife.

CULTURAL AND HISTORICAL LANDMARKS

Lake Tahoe is home to numerous cultural and historical landmarks that offer a glimpse into the region's rich past. These sites are cherished by both locals and visitors, serving as reminders of the area's diverse heritage.

- **Vikingsholm:** Located in Emerald Bay, Vikingsholm is a stunning example of Scandinavian architecture. Built in 1929 as a summer home for Lora Knight, Vikingsholm is now a museum open to the public. The mansion's intricate design and its picturesque setting make it one of the most iconic landmarks in Lake Tahoe.

- **Tallac Historic Site:** Situated on the south shore, the Tallac Historic Site features three estates that once belonged to wealthy families during the early 20th century. The site offers guided tours, cultural events, and exhibits that highlight the region's history as a summer retreat for the elite.

- **Donner Memorial State Park:** Located near Truckee, this park commemorates the tragic Donner Party, a group of pioneers who became trapped by snow during the winter of 1846-47. The park's museum and monument provide insight into the challenges faced by early settlers and the westward expansion of the United States.

ENVIRONMENTAL CONSERVATION AND SUSTAINABILITY

Lake Tahoe's pristine beauty has always been one of its most valuable assets, and efforts to protect and preserve the environment have been ongoing for decades. The lake's clarity and the surrounding wilderness are protected through various conservation initiatives.

- **The League to Save Lake Tahoe:** Established in 1957, this organization, also known by its slogan "Keep Tahoe Blue," has been instrumental in advocating for the protection of Lake Tahoe's environment. Their work includes combating pollution, promoting sustainable development, and preserving the lake's natural beauty.

- **Tahoe Regional Planning Agency (TRPA):** Formed in 1969, the TRPA is a bi-state agency that oversees land use and development in the Lake Tahoe Basin. Their mission is to balance the needs of the environment with those of the community, ensuring that the region remains sustainable for future generations.

- **Sustainable Tourism:** In recent years, there has been a growing emphasis on sustainable tourism in Lake Tahoe. Local businesses and organizations are increasingly focused on minimizing their environmental impact, whether through green building practices, waste reduction, or promoting eco-friendly activities for visitors.

CULTURAL TRADITIONS AND MODERN-DAY COMMUNITY

Lake Tahoe's cultural fabric is woven from its diverse history and the people who have called this region home over the centuries. Today, Lake Tahoe is a vibrant community where the past and present coexist harmoniously.

- **Local Festivals:** Lake Tahoe hosts a variety of cultural festivals throughout the year, celebrating everything from art and music to food and wine. The Lake Tahoe Shakespeare Festival at Sand Harbor is a highlight of the summer, offering performances in a stunning outdoor setting.

- **Art and Music:** The region is home to a thriving arts scene, with galleries, live music venues, and cultural events that showcase local talent. From art walks in Tahoe City to live performances at the Crystal Bay Club, there's always something to experience.

- **Community Spirit:** Despite its popularity as a tourist destination, Lake Tahoe retains a strong sense of community. Residents are passionate about preserving the natural environment and maintaining the unique character of the region. Local organizations, volunteer groups, and community events all contribute to the region's close-knit atmosphere.

2.3 LOCAL TRADITIONS AND FESTIVALS

The region is home to a variety of local traditions and festivals that celebrate everything from its historical roots to its modern-day artistic spirit. Whether you're visiting in the summer, winter, or any season in between, there's likely a festival or event that will immerse you in the local culture and traditions of Lake Tahoe.

1. LAKE TAHOE SHAKESPEARE FESTIVAL

- **When:** July - August

- **Where:** Sand Harbor, Nevada

One of the most iconic cultural events in Lake Tahoe is the Lake Tahoe Shakespeare Festival, held annually at the scenic Sand Harbor State Park. This festival brings the timeless works of William Shakespeare to life in an open-air amphitheater set against the backdrop of Lake Tahoe's shimmering waters. The combination of professional theater, breathtaking scenery, and the magic of Shakespeare's plays makes this event a must-see for both locals and visitors.

The festival not only showcases Shakespearean classics but also features contemporary plays and musical performances. Attendees can enjoy a picnic on the beach before the show or indulge in gourmet food and wine available at the venue. It's a cultural experience that perfectly blends art, nature, and community.

2. SNOWFEST!

- **When:** Late February - Early March

- **Where:** North Lake Tahoe

SnowFest! is a beloved winter tradition in North Lake Tahoe that has been celebrated for over 40 years. This 10-day festival is a joyous celebration of all things winter, featuring a variety of events that bring the community together for fun and entertainment. From parades and fireworks to snow sculpting contests and polar bear swims, SnowFest! offers something for everyone.

One of the highlights of the festival is the annual Polar Bear Swim, where brave participants take a plunge into the icy waters of Lake Tahoe. Other popular events include the SnowFest! Parade, which showcases local floats, marching bands, and lively performers, and the annual Gar Woods Polar Bear Swim, a favorite for thrill-seekers. The festival is a wonderful way to experience the local spirit and camaraderie that defines the Lake Tahoe community.

3. VALHALLA ART, MUSIC & THEATRE FESTIVAL

- **When:** June - September

- **Where:** Tallac Historic Site, South Lake Tahoe

The Valhalla Art, Music & Theatre Festival is a summer-long celebration of the arts, held at the historic Valhalla Estate at the Tallac Historic Site. This festival offers a diverse lineup of performances, including live theater, music concerts, art exhibits, and workshops, all set against the picturesque backdrop of Lake Tahoe's south shore.

Valhalla's Grand Hall, with its rustic charm and stunning lake views, serves as the main venue for many of the festival's events. The festival is a unique opportunity to enjoy world-class performances in an intimate and historic setting. It's also a great way to explore the Tallac Historic Site, with its beautifully preserved estates and gardens.

4. OKTOBERFEST AT CAMP RICHARDSON

- **When:** Late September - Early October

- **Where:** Camp Richardson Historic Resort and Marina, South Lake Tahoe

Lake Tahoe's version of Oktoberfest is a family-friendly celebration held at the Camp Richardson Historic Resort and Marina. This annual event captures the spirit of the traditional German festival with a local twist, offering a fun-filled weekend of live music, beer, brats, and Bavarian-themed activities.

Visitors can enjoy authentic German cuisine, including bratwurst, pretzels, and schnitzel, while sipping on locally brewed beers and listening to live polka bands. The festival also features a beer garden, a pumpkin patch, and a variety of games and contests, such as the popular beer stein holding competition. It's a festive way to welcome the fall season in Lake Tahoe.

5. GREAT GATSBY FESTIVAL

- **When:** August

- **Where:** Tallac Historic Site, South Lake Tahoe

Step back in time to the Roaring Twenties at the Great Gatsby Festival, held annually at the Tallac Historic Site. This event celebrates the glamour and style of the 1920s, with a focus on the history of the Tallac Resort, a popular destination for the wealthy during that era.

Attendees are encouraged to dress in period attire and participate in activities such as vintage car shows, fashion shows, and guided tours of the historic estates. The festival also features live jazz music, dance performances, and a speakeasy-themed cocktail party. The Great Gatsby Festival is a unique way to experience the elegance and charm of Lake Tahoe's past.

6. SAMPLE THE SIERRA

- **When:** Early September

- **Where:** Bijou Community Park, South Lake Tahoe

Sample the Sierra is a farm-to-fork festival that celebrates the rich agricultural heritage of the Sierra Nevada region. Held in early September, this event showcases the best of local food, wine, and art, with a focus on sustainability and supporting local producers.

The festival features tastings from local restaurants, wineries, and breweries, along with cooking demonstrations, live music, and a marketplace where visitors can purchase locally made products. Sample the Sierra is a wonderful opportunity to experience the flavors of Lake Tahoe and the surrounding area, while also supporting local farmers, chefs, and artisans.

7. AMERICA'S MOST BEAUTIFUL BIKE RIDE

- **When:** June

- **Where:** Around Lake Tahoe

America's Most Beautiful Bike Ride is an annual cycling event that takes participants on a scenic 72-mile loop around Lake Tahoe. The ride, which attracts cyclists from around the world, is renowned for its breathtaking views and challenging terrain.

The event offers several route options, including shorter rides for less experienced cyclists. Along the way, participants are treated to panoramic views of the lake, snow-capped peaks, and lush forests. The ride is also a fundraiser for the Leukemia & Lymphoma Society, adding a charitable aspect to the experience. Whether you're a seasoned cyclist or a casual rider, this event is a fantastic way to explore the beauty of Lake Tahoe on two wheels.

8. TAHOE CITY WINE WALK

- **When:** June

- **Where:** Tahoe City, North Shore

The Tahoe City Wine Walk is a popular summer event that combines wine tasting with a leisurely stroll through the charming town of Tahoe City. Held annually in June, the Wine Walk features tastings from local wineries, paired with small bites from Tahoe City's restaurants and shops.

Participants receive a commemorative wine glass and map of the tasting locations, allowing them to explore at their own pace. Along the way, they can enjoy live music, browse local art, and take in the stunning views of Lake Tahoe. The Tahoe City Wine Walk is a delightful way to spend a summer afternoon, experiencing the flavors and culture of the North Shore.

9. LIGHTS ON THE LAKE FIREWORKS

- **When:** July 4th

- **Where:** South Lake Tahoe

Lake Tahoe's Lights on the Lake Fireworks show is one of the largest and most spectacular Independence Day celebrations in the United States. Each year on July 4th, thousands of visitors gather along the shores of South Lake Tahoe to watch the sky light up in a dazzling display of fireworks.

The show is synchronized to music, which can be heard on local radio stations, creating a truly immersive experience. The best viewing spots include Nevada Beach, Edgewood Tahoe, and the Tahoe Queen paddlewheel boat. The Lights on the Lake Fireworks is a must-see event for anyone visiting Lake Tahoe during the summer.

10. LABOR DAY WEEKEND FIREWORKS EXTRAVAGANZA

- **When:** Labor Day Weekend

- **Where:** Kings Beach, North Shore

To mark the end of summer, the North Shore hosts the Labor Day Weekend Fireworks Extravaganza in Kings Beach. This festive event features a stunning fireworks display over the lake, drawing crowds of locals and visitors alike.

The fireworks are launched from barges on the lake, creating a beautiful reflection on the water. In addition to the fireworks, the weekend is filled with live music, beach games, and family-friendly activities. It's a perfect way to celebrate the final days of summer in Lake Tahoe.

2.4 Must-Know Local Etiquette

When visiting Lake Tahoe, it's important to be aware of and respect the local customs and etiquette to ensure that your trip is enjoyable and that you leave a positive impression on the community. Here's a guide to the must-know local etiquette for visitors to Lake Tahoe.

1. Respect the Environment

Lake Tahoe is renowned for its pristine natural beauty, and locals are passionate about preserving it. Whether you're hiking, boating, or simply enjoying the scenery, it's essential to follow the principles of Leave No Trace:

- **Pack It In, Pack It Out:** Always take your trash with you, and make sure to dispose of it properly. This includes food wrappers, bottles, and even organic waste like fruit peels.

- **Stay on Marked Trails:** When hiking or biking, stick to designated trails to protect the surrounding vegetation and prevent erosion.

- **Avoid Disturbing Wildlife:** Observe animals from a distance and do not feed them. Feeding wildlife can disrupt their natural behaviors and pose risks to both animals and humans.

- **Respect Fire Regulations:** Lake Tahoe is a wildfire-prone area. Always follow local fire regulations, which may include restrictions on campfires, fireworks, and smoking in certain areas.

2. Drive Safely and Courteously

Lake Tahoe's roads can be winding, narrow, and busy, especially during peak seasons. Safe and courteous driving is essential for everyone's safety and enjoyment:

- **Observe Speed Limits:** Speed limits in the Lake Tahoe area are strictly enforced, especially in residential and pedestrian-heavy areas. Drive slowly and cautiously, particularly in snowy or icy conditions.

- **Use Chains in Winter:** If you're driving during the winter, be prepared to use tire chains or snow tires. Roads can become slippery, and chains may be required on certain routes.

- **Yield to Pedestrians and Cyclists:** Many locals and visitors explore Lake Tahoe on foot or by bike. Always yield to pedestrians at crosswalks and give cyclists plenty of space.

- **Avoid Blocking Traffic:** Parking can be challenging in popular areas. If you can't find a spot, be patient and avoid stopping in traffic lanes or double parking.

3. BE MINDFUL OF NOISE LEVELS

Lake Tahoe is a peaceful, natural retreat for both residents and visitors. Maintaining a quiet environment, especially in residential areas, is greatly appreciated:

- **Limit Noise in Quiet Zones:** Areas near lakes, parks, and residential neighborhoods often have quiet hours. Avoid loud music, shouting, or other disturbances, especially early in the morning or late at night.

- **Respect Wildlife:** Keep noise levels down when hiking or exploring natural areas to avoid disturbing wildlife and other visitors seeking a tranquil experience.

- **Consider Neighbors in Accommodations:** If you're staying in a vacation rental or hotel, be considerate of your neighbors. Keep noise to a minimum, particularly during late-night hours.

4. SUPPORT LOCAL BUSINESSES

Lake Tahoe's economy relies heavily on tourism, and supporting local businesses is a great way to contribute to the community:

- **Shop Local:** Whenever possible, purchase goods from local shops, markets, and artisans. This helps sustain the local economy and provides you with unique, region-specific products.

- **Dine at Local Restaurants:** Lake Tahoe is home to a wide variety of restaurants that use fresh, local ingredients. Eating at local establishments helps support the community and gives you a taste of the region's culinary offerings.

- **Respect Service Workers:** Be courteous and respectful to service workers, including waitstaff, retail employees, and guides. Tipping is customary in the U.S., and a 15-20% tip is generally expected in restaurants.

5. UNDERSTAND AND FOLLOW LOCAL CUSTOMS

Every region has its own set of customs and social norms. In Lake Tahoe, these often revolve around outdoor activities and community spirit:

- **Greeting Others:** In smaller towns and on trails, it's common to greet others with a smile or a friendly "hello." This simple gesture reflects the welcoming nature of the Lake Tahoe community.

- **Outdoor Etiquette:** When engaging in outdoor activities, be considerate of others. For example, when on hiking trails, allow faster hikers to pass, and if you're taking a break, step off the trail to let others by.

- **Respect Property Boundaries:** Many areas around Lake Tahoe are private property, including some lakeside beaches. Always respect posted signs and avoid trespassing on private land.

6. PARTICIPATE IN LOCAL CONSERVATION EFFORTS

Lake Tahoe is a leader in environmental conservation, and visitors are encouraged to get involved:

- **Join a Clean-Up:** Many local organizations host beach and trail clean-up events. Participating in these activities is a great way to give back to the community and help preserve Lake Tahoe's natural beauty.

- **Choose Eco-Friendly Activities:** Opt for eco-friendly tours and activities that minimize environmental impact. Many local businesses offer sustainable options, from kayaking and hiking to eco-tours that focus on environmental education.

- **Reduce Plastic Use:** Bring a reusable water bottle, shopping bags, and containers to minimize plastic waste. Many businesses in Lake Tahoe support efforts to reduce plastic use and appreciate visitors who do the same.

7. BE AWARE OF LOCAL REGULATIONS

Lake Tahoe has specific rules and regulations that help maintain safety and preserve the environment. Familiarize yourself with these before your visit:

- **Wildlife Protection:** Feeding bears or leaving food accessible is illegal and dangerous. Secure all food and trash when camping or staying in cabins, and never approach or feed wildlife.

- **Fishing Regulations:** If you plan to fish, make sure you have the appropriate fishing license and are aware of local fishing regulations, including catch limits and protected species.

- **Camping Permits:** If you're camping, especially in backcountry areas, you may need a permit. Check with local authorities or park services before setting up camp.

8. ENJOY THE COMMUNITY SPIRIT

Lake Tahoe is known for its strong sense of community and the welcoming nature of its residents. Visitors are encouraged to embrace this spirit:

- **Participate in Local Events:** Attend local festivals, markets, and events to experience the culture and connect with residents. These gatherings are a great way to meet people and learn more about the area.

- **Respect Cultural and Historical Sites:** Many places around Lake Tahoe have cultural or historical significance, particularly to the Washoe Tribe. Treat these sites with respect, and follow any posted guidelines or restrictions.

CHAPTER 3: EXPLORING SOUTH LAKE TAHOE

3.1 HEAVENLY VILLAGE: SHOPPING, DINING, AND ENTERTAINMENT

Heavenly Village, located in the heart of South Lake Tahoe, is a vibrant hub of activity that offers a perfect blend of shopping, dining, and entertainment. Nestled at the base of the Heavenly Mountain Resort, this bustling village is a must-visit destination for anyone looking to experience the best of South Lake Tahoe's lively atmosphere. Whether you're a shopper, a foodie, or just looking for some fun, Heavenly Village has something for everyone.

SHOPPING AT HEAVENLY VILLAGE

Heavenly Village is a shopper's paradise, offering a wide variety of stores that cater to all tastes and interests. From outdoor gear to unique gifts and fashion, the village has everything you need to indulge in some retail therapy.

- **Outdoor and Sports Gear:** For those who want to hit the slopes or explore the great outdoors, Heavenly Village is home to several shops offering top-quality gear and apparel. Stores like **Heavenly Sports** and **The North Face** provide everything from ski and snowboard equipment to hiking boots and activewear, ensuring you're well-equipped for any adventure.

- **Fashion and Accessories:** If you're looking to update your wardrobe or find that perfect accessory, Heavenly Village has you covered. **Apparel shops** such as **Sessions** and **Rip N' Willies** offer a variety of trendy clothing and accessories, while **Sunglass Hut** provides a wide selection of stylish eyewear to protect your eyes from the Tahoe sun.

- **Unique Gifts and Souvenirs:** For those who want to bring home a piece of Tahoe, the village is filled with charming boutiques offering unique gifts and souvenirs. **Lake Tahoe Photo Gallery** is a great place to find stunning photographs of the region, while **Up Shirt Creek** offers a fun selection of Tahoe-themed clothing and gifts. **The Sock Spot** is a quirky shop specializing in unique and colorful socks that make great souvenirs.

- **Art and Home Decor:** If you're in search of something special for your home, **Pacific Crest Gallery** features a beautiful collection of fine art, jewelry, and home decor items. The gallery showcases works from local and regional artists, making it a perfect spot to find a one-of-a-kind piece.

DINING AT HEAVENLY VILLAGE

Heavenly Village is a food lover's dream, offering a diverse array of dining options that cater to every palate. Whether you're in the mood for a quick bite, a gourmet meal, or something sweet, the village's restaurants and cafes have it all.

- **Casual Dining:** For those looking for a relaxed meal, Heavenly Village offers a variety of casual dining spots. **Base Camp Pizza Co.** is a popular choice, known for its delicious pizzas, fresh salads, and lively outdoor patio. **California Burger Co.** is another favorite, offering gourmet burgers, craft beers, and live music in a fun, laid-back atmosphere.

- **Fine Dining:** If you're in the mood for something more upscale, **Kalani's** provides an elegant dining experience with a menu that blends Pacific Rim cuisine with fresh, local ingredients. **Azul Latin Kitchen** offers a vibrant, modern take on Latin American flavors, with a focus on organic and sustainable ingredients. Both restaurants provide a sophisticated ambiance perfect for a romantic dinner or special occasion.

- **Quick Bites and Snacks:** For a quick snack or a sweet treat, **Heavenly Village** has plenty of options. **Nestle Toll House Café** offers freshly baked cookies, brownies, and ice cream, making it a great spot to satisfy your sweet tooth. **Cinnabon** is another go-to for indulgent cinnamon rolls and other baked goods. If you need a caffeine fix, **Starbucks** and **Peet's Coffee** are conveniently located in the village.

- **Après-Ski Hot Spots:** After a day on the slopes, Heavenly Village is the perfect place to unwind with a drink. **Fire + Ice Grill and Bar** is a lively spot for après-ski, offering a unique "create-your-own" dining experience along with a full bar. **Gunbarrel Tavern & Eatery** is another great option, featuring craft cocktails, local beers, and a cozy outdoor fire pit where you can relax and soak in the village atmosphere.

ENTERTAINMENT AT HEAVENLY VILLAGE

Heavenly Village is not just about shopping and dining; it's also a hub for entertainment and fun, offering a variety of activities and events throughout the year.

- **Heavenly Village Cinemas:** Catch the latest blockbuster or an indie film at the **Heavenly Village Cinemas**. With multiple screens and comfortable seating, it's the perfect place to relax and enjoy a movie after a day of exploring. The theater regularly shows a mix of new releases, family-friendly films, and special screenings.

- **Ice Skating:** In the winter months, the **Heavenly Village Ice Rink** becomes a favorite spot for both locals and visitors. The outdoor rink, located in the heart of the village, is surrounded by twinkling lights and festive decorations, creating a magical winter wonderland. Skates can be rented on-site, making it easy for everyone to join in the fun.

- **Live Music and Events:** Heavenly Village regularly hosts live music and events, adding to the lively atmosphere. From local bands playing at the village's restaurants and bars to outdoor concerts and seasonal festivals, there's always something happening. The **Heavenly Village Summer Concert Series** is a highlight, offering free live music performances on weekends during the summer months.

- **Gondola Rides:** One of the most iconic experiences in Heavenly Village is taking a ride on the **Heavenly Gondola**. The gondola offers stunning panoramic views of Lake Tahoe and the surrounding mountains, making it a must-do for any visitor. In winter, it's the gateway to Heavenly Mountain Resort's ski slopes, while in summer, it provides access to hiking trails and the **Tamarack Lodge** at the top, where you can enjoy a meal with a view.

- **Miniature Golf and Family Fun:** For family-friendly entertainment, **Heavenly Village** offers a variety of activities, including a **miniature golf course** that's open during the warmer months. The course is designed with a Tahoe theme, making it a fun and engaging experience for all ages.

- **Seasonal Events:** Heavenly Village hosts a variety of seasonal events throughout the year, including the **Winter Holiday Tree Lighting Ceremony**, **Halloween Carnival**, and **Labor Day Weekend festivities**. These events often include live music, games, and activities for the whole family, making the village a lively and festive place to visit year-round.

3.2 SKI RESORTS: WINTER SPORTS AND ADVENTURE

The combination of stunning alpine scenery, diverse terrain, and excellent snow conditions makes Lake Tahoe a winter wonderland for skiers, snowboarders, and adventure seekers of all levels. Whether you're a seasoned pro or a beginner hitting the slopes for the first time, the ski resorts around Lake Tahoe provide a perfect setting for unforgettable winter adventures. Here's a guide to the top ski resorts in the area and what they have to offer.

1. HEAVENLY MOUNTAIN RESORT

Location: South Lake Tahoe, California/Nevada
Elevation: 10,067 feet (3,068 meters)
Skiable Terrain: 4,800 acres
Runs: 97
Lifts: 28

Overview:

Heavenly Mountain Resort is one of the largest and most popular ski resorts in Lake Tahoe, offering breathtaking views of both Lake Tahoe and the Nevada desert. Straddling the California-Nevada border, Heavenly is known for its diverse terrain, ranging from wide-open groomers to challenging tree runs and steep chutes.

Winter Sports and Activities:

- **Skiing and Snowboarding:** With nearly 100 runs spread across 4,800 acres, Heavenly has something for everyone. Beginners can enjoy the gentle slopes near the California Lodge, while advanced skiers and snowboarders can tackle the steep terrain on the Nevada side, including the legendary Mott and Killebrew Canyons.

- **Night Skiing:** Heavenly is one of the few resorts in Lake Tahoe that offers night skiing. The illuminated runs provide a unique experience, allowing you to extend your day on the slopes.

- **Terrain Parks:** Heavenly features several terrain parks designed for all skill levels, including jumps, rails, and boxes. The High Roller Terrain Park is the most advanced, attracting freestyle enthusiasts with its challenging features.

- **Gondola Rides:** The Heavenly Gondola offers more than just a ride to the top of the mountain. The 2.4-mile journey provides stunning panoramic views of Lake Tahoe, and you can stop at the Observation Deck for photos or a snack.

- **Snowshoeing and Tubing:** For those looking for activities off the slopes, Heavenly offers snowshoeing trails and a tubing hill at the top of the gondola, providing fun for the whole family.

Après-Ski:

Heavenly's après-ski scene is vibrant and varied, with plenty of options to relax and unwind after a day on the mountain. The **Tamarack Lodge** at the top of the gondola is a popular spot for a drink with a view, while the **Unbuckle at Tamarack** party is known for its lively atmosphere, complete with DJs, dancers, and drink specials. Down in Heavenly Village, you'll find a wide range of bars and restaurants, perfect for continuing the après-ski fun.

2. SQUAW VALLEY ALPINE MEADOWS

Location: Olympic Valley, California
Elevation: 9,050 feet (2,758 meters)
Skiable Terrain: 6,000 acres (combined)
Runs: 270+ (combined)
Lifts: 42 (combined)

Overview:

Squaw Valley Alpine Meadows, the largest ski resort in the Lake Tahoe area, is legendary for its challenging terrain and deep snowpack. Squaw Valley, the site of the 1960 Winter Olympics, is renowned for its steep slopes and technical runs, while Alpine Meadows offers a more laid-back vibe with wide-open bowls and pristine powder.

Winter Sports and Activities:

- **Skiing and Snowboarding:** With over 6,000 acres of skiable terrain between Squaw Valley and Alpine Meadows, this resort offers endless possibilities for exploration. Squaw Valley's challenging terrain includes steep chutes, big mountain lines, and advanced tree skiing, while Alpine Meadows is known for its scenic bowls and powder-filled meadows.

- **Terrain Parks:** Squaw Valley Alpine Meadows boasts some of the best terrain parks in the region, catering to all levels of freestyle skiers and snowboarders. The Mainline Park at Squaw Valley features large jumps and rails, while Alpine Meadows offers smaller, more beginner-friendly parks.

- **Guided Backcountry Tours:** For those seeking adventure beyond the groomed runs, Squaw Valley Alpine Meadows offers guided backcountry tours. These tours take you into the resort's vast backcountry terrain, where you can experience untracked powder and stunning alpine views.

- **Cross-Country Skiing and Snowshoeing:** The resort also offers extensive cross-country skiing and snowshoeing trails, allowing you to explore the beauty of the Sierra Nevada at a more relaxed pace.

Après-Ski:

The après-ski scene at Squaw Valley Alpine Meadows is lively and diverse. In Squaw Valley, the **Le Chamois & Loft Bar** is a legendary après-ski spot known for its laid-back vibe and outdoor deck. **Rocker@Squaw** is another popular choice, offering craft beers and comfort food in a casual setting. Alpine Meadows has a more relaxed après-ski atmosphere, with cozy lodges like **The Chalet** serving up hearty meals and warm drinks.

3. NORTHSTAR CALIFORNIA RESORT

Location: Truckee, California
Elevation: 8,610 feet (2,624 meters)
Skiable Terrain: 3,170 acres
Runs: 100
Lifts: 20

Overview:

NorthStar California Resort is known for its family-friendly atmosphere, luxury amenities, and impeccably groomed runs. The resort's combination of high-end accommodations, a charming village, and diverse terrain makes it a favorite among families and those seeking a more relaxed skiing experience.

Winter Sports and Activities:

- **Skiing and Snowboarding:** Northstar's terrain is ideal for beginners and intermediates, with wide, groomed runs and plenty of space to practice your skills. Advanced skiers will find challenging tree runs and black diamond trails on the backside of the mountain.

- **Terrain Parks:** Northstar is home to some of the best terrain parks in the Lake Tahoe area, including the Burton Progression Park, which is designed for beginners, and the more advanced Pinball Park, featuring jumps, rails, and halfpipes.

- **Cross-Country Skiing:** Northstar offers over 35 kilometers of groomed cross-country skiing trails, winding through serene forests and meadows. The resort's cross-country center provides rentals, lessons, and guided tours.

- **Ice Skating:** In the heart of the village, Northstar features a picturesque ice-skating rink surrounded by fire pits and cozy seating areas. It's a perfect spot for families to enjoy some off-slope fun.

Après-Ski:

Northstar's après-ski scene is sophisticated yet family-friendly. The **Village at Northstar** offers a variety of dining and shopping options, as well as live music and outdoor fire pits where you can relax with a hot chocolate or a glass of wine. **TC's Pub** is a popular spot for casual fare and craft beers, while **Ritz-Carlton Lake Tahoe** offers a more upscale après-ski experience with its **Highlands Bar** serving gourmet appetizers and signature cocktails.

4. KIRKWOOD MOUNTAIN RESORT

Location: Kirkwood, California
Elevation: 9,800 feet (2,987 meters)
Skiable Terrain: 2,300 acres
Runs: 86
Lifts: 15

Overview:
Kirkwood Mountain Resort is a hidden gem in the Lake Tahoe area, known for its deep powder, challenging terrain, and laid-back vibe. Located about 35 miles south of South Lake Tahoe, Kirkwood is a favorite among

advanced skiers and snowboarders who seek out its steep runs and abundant snowfall.

Winter Sports and Activities:

- **Skiing and Snowboarding:** Kirkwood is renowned for its expert terrain, including some of the steepest and most challenging runs in the Lake Tahoe area. The resort's unique topography creates natural bowls, cliffs, and chutes that provide endless opportunities for advanced skiers and snowboarders. However, there are also plenty of beginner and intermediate runs, making it accessible to all levels.

- **Backcountry Access:** Kirkwood is a gateway to some of the best backcountry skiing and snowboarding in the region. The resort offers guided tours and avalanche safety courses for those looking to explore beyond the resort's boundaries.

- **Cross-Country Skiing and Snowshoeing:** Kirkwood's cross-country center offers over 80 kilometers of groomed trails that wind through beautiful alpine forests and meadows. Snowshoeing is also a popular activity, with guided tours available for those who want to learn more about the area's natural environment.

Après-Ski:

Kirkwood's après-ski scene is more low-key compared to other Tahoe resorts, but it's perfect for those who appreciate a relaxed, mountain-town vibe. **The Kirkwood Inn & Saloon** is a historic spot offering hearty meals and a cozy atmosphere, ideal for warming up after a day on the slopes. For a more social setting, **The Wall Bar** at the base of the mountain offers craft beers, cocktails, and live music on weekends.

5. SIERRA-AT-TAHOE RESORT

Location: Twin Bridges, California
Elevation: 8,852 feet (2,698 meters)

Skiable Terrain: 2,000 acres
Runs: 46
Lifts: 14

Overview:
Sierra-at-Tahoe is a laid-back, family-friendly resort that offers a great mix of terrain, excellent snow, and a welcoming atmosphere. Located just 12 miles from South Lake Tahoe, Sierra-at-Tahoe is known for its tree skiing, terrain parks, and friendly community vibe.

Winter Sports and Activities:

- **Skiing and Snowboarding:** Sierra-at-Tahoe offers a diverse range of terrain, from beginner slopes to challenging tree runs. The resort's west-facing aspect often means it receives a lot of snow, providing excellent powder days. The tree skiing at Sierra is some of the best in the region, with well-spaced trees and natural features.

- **Terrain Parks:** Sierra-at-Tahoe is home to some of the best terrain parks in the Lake Tahoe area, including the Broadway Park for beginners and the more advanced Smokey BoarderX course. The resort is also known for its excellent halfpipe.

- **Family Fun:** Sierra-at-Tahoe is a great choice for families, with a dedicated beginner area, excellent ski school, and a tubing hill that provides hours of fun for kids and adults alike.

Après-Ski:

Sierra-at-Tahoe's après-ski scene is casual and welcoming, with several options for relaxing after a day on the slopes. **Baja Grill** offers Mexican-inspired fare and a lively atmosphere, while **Tiki Bar** is a popular spot for enjoying a cold drink in the sun. The **Sierra Pub** is a cozy spot with a friendly vibe, perfect for winding down with a beer or hot chocolate.

3.3 EMERALD BAY STATE PARK: HIKING AND SCENIC VIEWS

Emerald Bay State Park is one of Lake Tahoe's most stunning and iconic destinations, known for its striking natural beauty, crystal-clear waters, and captivating views. Designated as a National Natural Landmark, this park offers visitors a chance to experience some of the most breathtaking scenery in the region, whether through hiking, boating, or simply enjoying the panoramic vistas. If you're planning a visit to Lake Tahoe, Emerald Bay State Park is a must-see, and here's everything you need to know about hiking and taking in the scenic views.

OVERVIEW OF EMERALD BAY STATE PARK

Emerald Bay is located on the southwestern shore of Lake Tahoe, approximately 12 miles from South Lake Tahoe. The bay's vibrant emerald-green waters are surrounded by rugged mountains and dense forests, creating a dramatic and picturesque landscape. At the center of the bay lies Fannette Island, the only island in Lake Tahoe, which adds to the park's unique charm.

The park is home to several attractions, including the historic Vikingsholm mansion, a 38-room estate built in 1929, and Eagle Falls, a stunning waterfall that cascades down the mountainside. With its diverse hiking trails, scenic overlooks, and abundant wildlife, Emerald Bay State Park offers an unforgettable experience for nature lovers and outdoor enthusiasts.

HIKING AT EMERALD BAY STATE PARK

Emerald Bay State Park features some of the best hiking trails in Lake Tahoe, ranging from easy walks to more challenging treks. Here are some of the top hikes in the park:

1. EAGLE FALLS TRAIL

Distance: 2 miles round trip (Lower Eagle Falls)
Difficulty: Easy to Moderate
Elevation Gain: 400 feet

Overview:
The Eagle Falls Trail is one of the most popular hikes in Emerald Bay State Park, offering stunning views of both the falls and the surrounding mountains. The trail begins at the Eagle Falls Trailhead, located just off Highway 89. It's a short but rewarding hike that takes you to Lower Eagle Falls, where you can see the water tumbling down the rocky cliffs into the bay below.

The trail continues up to Upper Eagle Falls and Eagle Lake, providing even more spectacular views. The hike to Eagle Lake is a bit more challenging, with a steeper ascent, but the reward is worth it. Eagle Lake is a serene alpine lake surrounded by granite peaks, offering a peaceful spot to rest and enjoy the scenery.

Highlights:

- The impressive cascade of Lower Eagle Falls.

- Panoramic views of Emerald Bay from the trail.

- The tranquil setting of Eagle Lake.

2. RUBICON TRAIL

Distance: 4.5 miles one way (Emerald Bay to D.L. Bliss State Park)
Difficulty: Moderate
Elevation Gain: 300 feet

Overview:
The Rubicon Trail is one of the most scenic hikes in Lake Tahoe, running along the western shore of the lake from Emerald Bay to D.L. Bliss State Park. This trail offers stunning, uninterrupted views of Lake Tahoe's deep blue waters, rocky cliffs, and lush forests. It's a relatively easy hike with gentle elevation changes, making it suitable for hikers of all levels.

Starting from Emerald Bay, the trail winds along the shoreline, passing through forests of pine and fir trees. You'll have plenty of opportunities to stop and take in the views, with several lookout points along the way. The trail also passes by Vikingsholm, so you can take a detour to explore the historic mansion and its surrounding gardens.

Highlights:

- Stunning lake views from multiple vantage points.

- Access to secluded beaches and coves along the trail.

- The opportunity to explore Vikingsholm and Fannette Island.

3. VIKINGSHOLM TRAIL

Distance: 1.7 miles round trip
Difficulty: Easy
Elevation Gain: 450 feet

Overview:
The Vikingsholm Trail is a short but steep hike that takes you from the parking lot at Highway 89 down to the shores of Emerald Bay and the historic Vikingsholm mansion. The trail descends through a forested area, with occasional views of the bay and surrounding mountains. While the hike back up can be strenuous, the walk down is relatively easy and offers beautiful scenery.

Once you reach the bottom, you can tour the Vikingsholm mansion, explore the shoreline, or take a short hike to Lower Eagle Falls. If you're feeling adventurous, you can rent a kayak or paddleboard to explore Emerald Bay and paddle out to Fannette Island.

Highlights:

- The historic Vikingsholm mansion, a stunning example of Scandinavian architecture.

- Access to the shores of Emerald Bay and Fannette Island.

- Beautiful views of the bay and surrounding forest.

4. BAYVIEW TRAIL

Distance: 2 miles round trip to Cascade Falls; 10 miles round trip to Maggie's Peak
Difficulty: Moderate to Difficult
Elevation Gain: 1,900 feet (to Maggie's Peak)

Overview:
The Bayview Trail offers two rewarding hiking options: a shorter hike to Cascade Falls and a longer, more challenging trek to Maggie's Peak. The trailhead is located at the Bayview Campground, just off Highway 89.

The hike to Cascade Falls is relatively short and easy, making it a great option for families. The trail leads to a viewpoint overlooking the falls, where you can see the water cascading down into Cascade Lake. For those looking for a more strenuous hike, continue on the trail to Maggie's Peak, which offers some of the best panoramic views in the area. From the summit, you can see Emerald Bay, Lake Tahoe, and the surrounding peaks.

Highlights:

- The picturesque Cascade Falls, set against a backdrop of granite cliffs.

- Sweeping views of Lake Tahoe and the Sierra Nevada from Maggie's Peak.

- A peaceful hike through dense forests and along mountain ridges.

SCENIC VIEWS AT EMERALD BAY STATE PARK

Emerald Bay State Park is renowned for its breathtaking vistas, which can be enjoyed from several lookout points and trails within the park. Here are some of the best spots to take in the views:

1. Inspiration Point

Location: Off Highway 89, above Emerald Bay

Overview:
Inspiration Point is one of the most popular viewpoints in Emerald Bay State Park, offering a panoramic view of the entire bay, including Fannette Island and the surrounding mountains. The lookout is easily accessible from the parking area and provides a stunning vantage point for photography and sightseeing. On a clear day, you can see the vibrant colors of the water, the lush green of the forest, and the snow-capped peaks in the distance.

2. Vikingsholm Overlook

Location: Off Highway 89, near the Vikingsholm Trailhead

Overview:

The Vikingsholm Overlook is another excellent viewpoint, located near the trailhead for the Vikingsholm Trail. This overlook provides a bird's-eye view of Vikingsholm, Fannette Island, and the sparkling waters of Emerald Bay. It's a great spot to take in the scenery before or after hiking down to the mansion.

3. Eagle Point

Location: On the southern tip of Emerald Bay, accessible via the Rubicon Trail

Overview:
Eagle Point offers a quieter, more secluded spot to enjoy the views of Emerald Bay. Located at the southern tip of the bay, this area can be accessed via the Rubicon Trail or by boat. From Eagle Point, you'll have a unique perspective of the bay, with the surrounding mountains framing the scene. It's a peaceful place to relax and take in the natural beauty of the area.

4. FANNETTE ISLAND

Location: In the middle of Emerald Bay, accessible by boat or kayak

Overview:
Fannette Island is the only island in Lake Tahoe and is located in the center of Emerald Bay. You can paddle out to the island by kayak or canoe and hike to the top, where you'll find the ruins of a small stone tea house. The views from the island are incredible, offering a 360-degree panorama of Emerald Bay and the surrounding mountains.

3.4 NIGHTLIFE AND CASINOS: AFTER-DARK FUN

Lake Tahoe offers a wide range of after-dark activities that cater to both those looking to party and those seeking a more relaxed evening. Here's a guide to the best nightlife and casino experiences in Lake Tahoe.

1. SOUTH LAKE TAHOE: THE HEART OF NIGHTLIFE AND CASINOS

South Lake Tahoe is the epicenter of nightlife in the region, offering a mix of casinos, nightclubs, bars, and entertainment venues that make it the go-to destination for after-dark fun.

CASINOS IN SOUTH LAKE TAHOE

South Lake Tahoe is home to several major casinos, all located on the Nevada side of the state line. These casinos are known for their lively atmosphere, offering everything from gaming and dining to live entertainment and nightclubs.

- **Harrah's Lake Tahoe:** Harrah's is one of the most iconic casinos in Lake Tahoe, offering a wide range of gaming options, including slot machines, table games, and a poker room. The casino also features the South Shore Room, a venue that hosts live performances from big-name artists and comedians. For nightlife, **Peek Nightclub** at

Harrah's is the place to be, offering a high-energy environment with top DJs, VIP bottle service, and a chic setting.

- **Harveys Lake Tahoe:** Connected to Harrah's by an underground walkway, Harveys is another top casino in South Lake Tahoe. Harveys offers an extensive gaming floor with slots, table games, and a poker room. The **Cabo Wabo Cantina** at Harveys, owned by rock legend Sammy Hagar, is a popular spot for live music, drinks, and casual dining. Harveys also hosts outdoor concerts during the summer at the Lake Tahoe Outdoor Arena, featuring top musical acts.

- **MontBleu Resort Casino & Spa:** MontBleu combines a stylish casino with a range of entertainment options. The casino floor features slots, table games, and a sports book, while the resort's nightlife offerings include the **Opal Ultra Lounge**, a trendy nightclub with a dance floor, DJ sets, and VIP areas. MontBleu is also home to **Blu Nightclub**, which hosts themed parties and live performances.

- **Hard Rock Hotel & Casino Lake Tahoe:** The Hard Rock Hotel & Casino brings the brand's signature rock 'n' roll vibe to Lake Tahoe. The casino offers a wide variety of gaming options, and the hotel is filled with music memorabilia. The **Vinyl Showroom** at Hard Rock is a great spot for live music, comedy, and other performances, while **Center Bar** is the perfect place to grab a drink and enjoy the lively atmosphere.

NIGHTCLUBS AND BARS IN SOUTH LAKE TAHOE

South Lake Tahoe's nightlife extends beyond the casinos, with a variety of bars and nightclubs that cater to different tastes and moods.

- **Xhale Lounge:** Located in the heart of South Lake Tahoe, Xhale Lounge is a stylish and modern hookah bar that transforms into a lively nightclub after dark. With a full bar, DJ music, and a dance floor, Xhale Lounge is a great spot for a night out with friends.

- **Whiskey Dick's Saloon:** For a more laid-back vibe, Whiskey Dick's Saloon offers a classic dive bar experience with live music, pool tables, and a wide selection of beers. The bar regularly hosts local and touring bands, making it a great place to catch live music in an unpretentious setting.

- **The Loft Theatre & Lounge:** Located in Heavenly Village, The Loft combines a theater, lounge, and restaurant in one venue. The Loft is known for its magic shows, which are popular with both locals and visitors. After the show, the lounge area offers a cozy spot to enjoy craft cocktails and tapas.

- **McP's Taphouse Grill:** A popular spot for locals and visitors alike, McP's Taphouse Grill offers live music every night, a wide selection of beers on tap, and hearty pub food. With a relaxed and friendly atmosphere, it's a great place to unwind after a day of exploring Lake Tahoe.

2. NORTH LAKE TAHOE: LAID-BACK VIBES AND LOCAL GEMS

While South Lake Tahoe is known for its bustling nightlife, North Lake Tahoe offers a more laid-back, intimate experience, with a focus on local bars and cozy lounges.

CASINOS IN NORTH LAKE TAHOE

- **Crystal Bay Casino:** Located on the Nevada side of the state line, Crystal Bay Casino is a favorite among locals and visitors for its classic gaming experience and live entertainment. The casino offers slots, table games, and a sports book, as well as the **Crown Room**, a venue that hosts live music, comedy, and other performances. The casino's **Red Room** is a popular late-night spot, offering DJ sets and a lively dance floor.

- **Hyatt Regency Lake Tahoe Resort, Spa and Casino:** Situated in Incline Village, the Hyatt Regency offers a more upscale casino experience. The casino features a range of gaming options, including slots, table games, and a poker room. The resort's **Cutthroat's Saloon** is a great spot for a casual drink, while the **Lone Eagle Grille** offers fine dining with stunning lake views.

BARS AND LOUNGES IN NORTH LAKE TAHOE

- **Lone Eagle Grille:** Located at the Hyatt Regency, the Lone Eagle Grille offers an upscale dining experience with a cozy, lodge-style ambiance. The bar area is perfect for enjoying a craft cocktail or glass of wine by the fireplace, with views of Lake Tahoe providing a stunning backdrop.

- **Gar Woods Grill & Pier:** Known for its lively atmosphere and stunning lakefront location, Gar Woods in Carnelian Bay is a popular spot for both daytime and nighttime fun. The restaurant and bar are famous for their signature "Wet Woody" cocktails, and during the summer, the outdoor deck is a great place to watch the sunset over the lake.

- **Pete 'n Peters:** A classic sports bar in Tahoe City, Pete 'n Peters is a local favorite known for its laid-back vibe, friendly staff, and a great selection of beers. It's the perfect place to catch a game, play some pool, and enjoy a cold drink with friends.

- **Jake's on the Lake:** Located in Tahoe City, Jake's on the Lake offers a relaxing lakeside dining experience with a bar that's perfect for enjoying a drink while taking in the views. The bar features a great selection of local beers, wines, and cocktails, and the outdoor seating area is a favorite during the warmer months.

3. ENTERTAINMENT AND LIVE MUSIC

Lake Tahoe's nightlife isn't just about bars and casinos—there's also a vibrant live music and entertainment scene that adds to the after-dark fun.

- **Lake Tahoe Outdoor Arena at Harveys:** This outdoor venue in South Lake Tahoe hosts some of the biggest names in music during the summer concert series. With the stunning backdrop of the

Sierra Nevada mountains, it's one of the most scenic places to catch a live show.

- **Crystal Bay Club Casino:** The Crystal Bay Club Casino is known for its live music events, featuring a diverse lineup of bands and artists throughout the year. The **Crown Room** and **Red Room** are the main venues, offering everything from rock and blues to electronic music.

- **The Loft Theatre & Lounge:** In addition to its magic shows, The Loft Theatre in Heavenly Village hosts live music and DJs in its lounge, creating a cozy and intimate atmosphere for a night out.

- **Winter Festivals and Events:** During the winter season, Lake Tahoe comes alive with festivals and events, many of which include nighttime activities. **SnowGlobe Music Festival** is a popular New Year's Eve event in South Lake Tahoe, featuring multiple stages, electronic music, and a high-energy crowd.

4. APRÈS-SKI HOTSPOTS

No discussion of nightlife in Lake Tahoe would be complete without mentioning the après-ski scene, which is an integral part of the culture here. After a day on the slopes, there's nothing better than relaxing with a drink and some good company.

- **Tamarack Lodge at Heavenly Mountain Resort:** Located at the top of the Heavenly Gondola, Tamarack Lodge is a popular spot for après-ski with stunning views, live music, and a lively atmosphere. The lodge's **Unbuckle at Tamarack** party is known for its DJs, dancers, and drink specials, making it a must-visit for those looking to continue the fun after the lifts close.

- **Le Chamois & Loft Bar at Squaw Valley:** A legendary après-ski spot in North Lake Tahoe, Le Chamois (affectionately known as "The Chammy") is where locals and visitors gather after a day on the slopes. With its casual vibe, cold beers, and outdoor deck, it's the perfect place to swap stories about the day's adventures.

- **Base Camp Pizza Co. in Heavenly Village:** This popular restaurant in Heavenly Village offers live music, craft beers, and delicious pizzas, making it a great spot for après-ski in South Lake Tahoe. The outdoor patio is heated and provides a cozy spot to relax after a day on the mountain.

CHAPTER 4: NORTH LAKE TAHOE ADVENTURES

4.1 KINGS BEACH: WATER SPORTS AND RELAXATION

Kings Beach, located on the northern shore of Lake Tahoe, is a charming and lively community that offers the perfect blend of outdoor adventure and relaxation. Known for its wide, sandy beaches and crystal-clear waters, Kings Beach is a top destination for visitors looking to enjoy water sports, beach activities, and the laid-back atmosphere that defines North Lake Tahoe. Whether you're seeking adrenaline-pumping fun on the water or a peaceful day soaking up the sun, Kings Beach has something for everyone.

OVERVIEW OF KINGS BEACH

Kings Beach is one of the largest and most popular beach areas on the North Shore of Lake Tahoe. The town's main attraction is its expansive public beach, which stretches for over a mile along the shoreline, offering stunning views of the lake and the surrounding Sierra Nevada mountains. The beach is family-friendly and equipped with all the amenities you need for a day of fun in the sun, including picnic tables, restrooms, and playgrounds.

The town itself has a relaxed, bohemian vibe, with a variety of local shops, cafes, and restaurants lining the streets. Kings Beach is also conveniently located near several hiking trails and other outdoor attractions, making it an ideal base for exploring North Lake Tahoe.

WATER SPORTS AT KINGS BEACH

Kings Beach is a haven for water sports enthusiasts, offering a wide range of activities that cater to all skill levels. Whether you're looking to paddle across the serene waters of Lake Tahoe, zip across the surface on a jet ski, or explore the underwater world while snorkeling, Kings Beach has it all.

1. STAND-UP PADDLEBOARDING (SUP)

Overview:
Stand-up paddleboarding is one of the most popular activities at Kings Beach, thanks to the calm, clear waters of Lake Tahoe. SUP offers a fantastic way to explore the shoreline, get some exercise, and enjoy the beautiful scenery. The shallow waters near the beach are perfect for beginners, while more experienced paddlers can venture further out to discover hidden coves and secluded spots.

Where to Rent: Several local shops near Kings Beach offer paddleboard rentals and lessons. **Tahoe Paddle & Oar** is a popular choice, providing high-quality paddleboards and expert instruction for those new to the sport. Rentals typically include life jackets and paddles, and guided tours are also available for those looking to explore the lake with a knowledgeable guide.

2. KAYAKING

Overview: Kayaking is another fantastic way to experience Lake Tahoe's stunning waters. Kings Beach is an ideal starting point for a kayaking adventure, with plenty of opportunities to paddle along the shoreline or venture out to explore nearby attractions like Crystal Bay or the rocky outcrops around Speedboat Beach. The calm waters make kayaking accessible for all ages and skill levels, and it's a great way to get up close to the lake's natural beauty.

Where to Rent: Like paddleboarding, kayaking rentals are widely available at Kings Beach. **Adrift Tahoe** offers single and tandem kayak rentals, as well as guided tours that take you to some of the most scenic spots on the lake. Kayak rentals come with all the necessary gear, including paddles and life jackets.

3. JET SKIING

Overview: For those looking for a more adrenaline-pumping activity, jet skiing at Kings Beach offers an exhilarating way to explore Lake Tahoe. Zoom across the surface of the lake at high speeds, feel the wind in your hair, and take in the breathtaking views of the surrounding mountains. Jet skiing is a thrilling way to experience the vastness of Lake Tahoe, and it's perfect for adventure seekers.

Where to Rent: Jet ski rentals are available from several vendors in Kings Beach. **North Tahoe Watersports** is a popular option, offering a fleet of well-maintained jet skis for hourly or daily rental. They also provide safety instructions and life jackets, ensuring that you can enjoy your ride with confidence.

4. PARASAILING

Overview: For a bird's-eye view of Lake Tahoe, parasailing is an unforgettable experience. Soar high above the water and take in panoramic views of the lake, the surrounding mountains, and the forested shoreline. Parasailing at Kings Beach is a safe and exciting adventure that provides a unique perspective on the beauty of Lake Tahoe.

Where to Go: Parasailing services are offered by several companies in Kings Beach, including **North Tahoe Watersports**. They provide tandem or solo flights, and experienced crew members ensure a smooth and enjoyable ride. Parasailing is suitable for most ages, and no prior experience is required.

5. SNORKELING AND SWIMMING

Overview: Kings Beach's clear, shallow waters are perfect for swimming and snorkeling. The sandy bottom and gentle slope into deeper water make it an ideal spot for families and casual swimmers. For those interested in exploring beneath the surface, snorkeling offers a chance to see some of the lake's fish species and underwater rock formations. While Lake Tahoe's waters can be chilly, especially early in the season, the experience is refreshing and invigorating.

Tips:

Bring your own snorkeling gear or rent it from local shops. The best time for snorkeling is usually during the warmer months of July and August when the water temperature is more comfortable.

RELAXATION AT KINGS BEACH

While Kings Beach is a hub for water sports, it's also an excellent place to unwind and enjoy some relaxation. The wide, sandy beach and beautiful surroundings make it a perfect spot for a leisurely day by the water.

1. SUNBATHING AND PICNICKING

Overview: With its spacious sandy shores and stunning views, Kings Beach is an ideal place for sunbathing and picnicking. Lay out a blanket, soak up the sun, and enjoy the peaceful atmosphere. The beach is equipped with picnic tables and BBQ grills, so you can easily enjoy a meal with family or friends. Pack a picnic or pick up some food from one of the local eateries, and enjoy a relaxing day by the lake.

Tip:

Arrive early during peak summer months to secure a good spot, as Kings Beach can get busy, especially on weekends.

2. BEACH YOGA

Overview:

Beach yoga is a popular activity at Kings Beach, offering a serene way to start or end your day. With the calming sound of the waves and the stunning backdrop of Lake Tahoe, practicing yoga on the beach is both rejuvenating and grounding. Many local instructors offer group classes on the sand, allowing you to connect with the natural beauty of the area while improving your flexibility and mindfulness.

Where to Join: Look for flyers or check local yoga studios in Kings Beach for class schedules. Classes are often held in the morning or evening when the beach is less crowded and the temperatures are cooler.

3. Exploring the Local Shops and Cafés

Overview:
After a day of water sports or lounging on the beach, take some time to explore the local shops and cafés that give Kings Beach its unique charm. The town is home to a variety of boutique stores selling everything from beachwear and souvenirs to locally-made crafts and art. Strolling through the town is a relaxing way to spend an afternoon, and you're sure to find something special to take home.

Cafés and Dining: Kings Beach has a range of dining options, from casual beachside cafes to more upscale restaurants. **Log Cabin Café & Ice Cream** is a local favorite for breakfast and lunch, offering hearty meals and delicious desserts. For a more refined dining experience, **The Soule Domain** offers a cozy atmosphere and a menu focused on fresh, locally-sourced ingredients. Grab a coffee or smoothie at **Java Hut** before heading back to the beach for more relaxation.

4. Evening Beach Bonfires

Overview:
As the sun sets over Lake Tahoe, Kings Beach becomes a tranquil and magical place to be. Many visitors enjoy gathering around a beach bonfire, sharing stories, roasting marshmallows, and taking in the starry sky. Bonfires are a wonderful way to end a day at the lake, creating memories that will last long after your visit.

Tips:
Check local regulations before starting a bonfire, as fire restrictions may be in place during certain times of the year. Some parts of Kings Beach may have designated fire pits available for use.

5. WATCHING THE SUNSET

Overview:
Kings Beach is renowned for its spectacular sunsets. As the day draws to a close, the sky over Lake Tahoe lights up in shades of pink, orange, and purple, reflecting off the water in a dazzling display. Watching the sunset from Kings Beach is a peaceful and awe-inspiring experience, and it's the perfect way to conclude your day of adventure and relaxation.

Best Spots: Find a comfortable spot on the beach or at one of the nearby parks to watch the sunset. If you're on the water, paddleboarding or kayaking during sunset offers a truly magical perspective.

4.2 INCLINE VILLAGE: LUXURY RESORTS AND GOLFING

Nestled on the serene north shore of Lake Tahoe, Incline Village is a premier destination for those seeking a luxurious escape in one of the most beautiful regions of the Sierra Nevada. Known for its upscale amenities, world-class golf courses, and stunning lakefront properties, Incline Village offers a perfect blend of relaxation and recreation. Whether you're a golf enthusiast looking to play on some of the finest courses in the area, or simply in need of a tranquil getaway in a luxury resort, Incline Village has everything you need for an unforgettable experience.

LUXURY RESORTS IN INCLINE VILLAGE

Incline Village is home to some of the most prestigious resorts in Lake Tahoe, offering a range of accommodations that cater to those seeking comfort, elegance, and a touch of indulgence. These resorts are known for their exceptional service, luxurious amenities, and breathtaking views of Lake Tahoe.

1. Hyatt Regency Lake Tahoe Resort, Spa and Casino

Overview:
The Hyatt Regency Lake Tahoe is the crown jewel of Incline Village, offering a blend of rustic elegance and modern luxury. This lakefront resort is set against the backdrop of the Sierra Nevada mountains, providing stunning views of Lake Tahoe. The resort's design incorporates natural materials like stone and wood, creating a cozy, lodge-like atmosphere that's both inviting and sophisticated.

Amenities:

- **Private Beach:** The resort features a private sandy beach where guests can relax, swim, or enjoy water sports.

- **Stillwater Spa:** The on-site spa offers a range of treatments designed to rejuvenate the body and mind, from massages and facials to body wraps and hydrotherapy.

- **Casino:** The resort's casino offers a variety of gaming options, including slot machines, table games, and a sports book.

- **Outdoor Pool and Hot Tubs:** The heated outdoor pool and hot tubs are open year-round, providing a perfect spot to unwind after a day of adventure.

- **Dining:** The Hyatt Regency offers several dining options, including the Lone Eagle Grille, which serves gourmet meals with panoramic views of the lake.

Why Stay Here: The Hyatt Regency Lake Tahoe is ideal for travelers seeking luxury with direct access to Lake Tahoe's natural beauty. Whether you're enjoying a spa day, relaxing on the beach, or trying your luck at the casino, this resort offers a comprehensive, high-end experience.

2. THE RITZ-CARLTON, LAKE TAHOE

Overview:
While technically located in nearby Truckee, The Ritz-Carlton, Lake Tahoe is close enough to Incline Village to be a convenient option for those seeking the ultimate in luxury. This five-star resort is nestled in the mountains and offers ski-in/ski-out access during the winter, as well as close proximity to Lake Tahoe's beaches in the summer.

Amenities:

- **Mountain Concierge:** The resort provides personalized concierge services to help plan outdoor activities, from skiing to hiking.

- **Spa:** The 17,000-square-foot spa offers an extensive menu of treatments, including massages, facials, and wellness rituals.

- **Fine Dining:** The resort's signature restaurant, Manzanita, offers a seasonal menu that blends classic techniques with a modern twist, all using locally sourced ingredients.

- **Pool and Hot Tubs:** The resort features a heated outdoor pool and multiple hot tubs, offering spectacular views of the mountains.

- **Exclusive Lake Club:** Guests have access to The Ritz-Carlton Lake Club on Lake Tahoe, where they can enjoy lakefront dining, water sports, and private beach access.

Why Stay Here: The Ritz-Carlton, Lake Tahoe is perfect for those who want the pinnacle of luxury and service, with easy access to both mountain and lake activities. The combination of world-class amenities and breathtaking natural surroundings makes it a top choice for discerning travelers.

3. CLUB TAHOE RESORT

Overview:
For a more intimate and relaxed experience, Club Tahoe Resort offers condo-style accommodations in a serene forest setting. This resort is ideal

for families and groups looking for spacious lodging with all the comforts of home, combined with the amenities of a luxury resort.

Amenities:

- **Fully Equipped Condos:** Each unit comes with a full kitchen, living room with a fireplace, and a private balcony or patio.

- **Recreation Center:** The resort features a recreation center with a pool, hot tub, sauna, and fitness center.

- **Tennis and Pickleball Courts:** Guests can enjoy on-site tennis and pickleball courts, perfect for some friendly competition.

- **Game Room and Lounge:** The resort's game room includes pool tables, arcade games, and a lounge area for relaxing.

- **Proximity to Golf:** Club Tahoe Resort is located close to Incline Village's golf courses, making it a convenient choice for golfers.

Why Stay Here: Club Tahoe Resort is ideal for travelers who want the flexibility of condo accommodations with resort-style amenities. It's a great option for families and groups who want a home-away-from-home experience with easy access to outdoor activities and golf.

GOLFING IN INCLINE VILLAGE

Incline Village is renowned for its world-class golf courses, which are set amidst the stunning scenery of Lake Tahoe. Whether you're an avid golfer or a casual player, the courses here offer a challenging yet rewarding experience, with meticulously maintained greens and breathtaking views at every turn.

1. INCLINE VILLAGE CHAMPIONSHIP GOLF COURSE

Overview:
The Incline Village Championship Golf Course is one of the premier golf destinations in Lake Tahoe, known for its challenging layout and stunning

views of the surrounding mountains and forest. Designed by the legendary Robert Trent Jones Sr., this par-72 course offers a true test of skill for golfers of all levels.

Course Features:

- **18-Hole Championship Course:** The course is known for its strategic design, featuring narrow fairways, water hazards, and well-placed bunkers.

- **Stunning Scenery:** Players are treated to panoramic views of the Sierra Nevada mountains and Lake Tahoe, with several holes offering particularly scenic vistas.

- **Pro Shop:** The on-site pro shop offers a wide selection of golf gear, apparel, and equipment, as well as club rentals.

- **Practice Facilities:** The course features a driving range, putting green, and chipping area, allowing players to warm up before their round.

- **Lessons and Clinics:** PGA-certified instructors are available for private lessons and group clinics, catering to golfers of all skill levels.

Why Play Here: The Incline Village Championship Golf Course is perfect for golfers who want a challenging and scenic round of golf in a beautiful setting. The course's design requires strategic thinking and precision, making it a rewarding experience for serious golfers.

2. INCLINE VILLAGE MOUNTAIN GOLF COURSE

Overview:
For those looking for a more relaxed and accessible round of golf, the Incline Village Mountain Golf Course offers a fun and scenic alternative. This 18-hole executive course is shorter than the Championship Course but still offers plenty of challenges, particularly with its elevation changes and undulating greens.

Course Features:

- **18-Hole Executive Course:** The Mountain Course is a par-58 layout, making it a quicker round that's ideal for families, beginners, and those with limited time.

- **Mountain Scenery:** The course winds through the forested hills of Incline Village, offering beautiful views and a peaceful atmosphere.

- **Casual Atmosphere:** The Mountain Course is known for its friendly and relaxed vibe, making it a great place to enjoy a round of golf with friends or family.

- **Clubhouse and Pro Shop:** The course has a small clubhouse and pro shop, where you can pick up snacks, drinks, and golf essentials.

Why Play Here: The Incline Village Mountain Golf Course is perfect for those looking for a fun and scenic round of golf without the intensity of a full-length course. It's an excellent choice for beginners, families, or anyone who wants to enjoy the beauty of Lake Tahoe while playing a more relaxed game.

OTHER ACTIVITIES IN INCLINE VILLAGE

While golf and luxury resorts are the main attractions in Incline Village, there's plenty more to do in this charming community.

- **Beaches:** Incline Village is home to several beautiful beaches, including **Burnt Cedar Beach** and **Incline Beach**, where you can swim, sunbathe, or enjoy water sports. These beaches are exclusive to residents and guests staying at certain properties, offering a more private and tranquil experience.

- **Hiking and Biking:** The area around Incline Village is crisscrossed with hiking and biking trails, including the popular **Flume Trail**, which offers stunning views of Lake Tahoe. Whether you're looking for a leisurely walk or a challenging hike, there's a trail to suit every level.

- **Tennis and Pickleball:** In addition to its golf courses, Incline Village offers top-notch tennis and pickleball facilities. The Incline Village Tennis Center features multiple courts and offers lessons, clinics, and tournaments.

- **Dining and Shopping:** Incline Village has a variety of dining options, from casual eateries to fine dining restaurants. **Lone Eagle Grille** is a standout, offering gourmet cuisine with panoramic lake views. The village also has several boutique shops where you can find everything from outdoor gear to unique gifts.

4.3 TAHOE CITY: HISTORIC SITES AND LAKESIDE STROLLS

Tahoe City, located on the northwestern shore of Lake Tahoe, is a charming and picturesque town that offers a unique blend of history, culture, and natural beauty. As one of the oldest communities in the Lake Tahoe region, Tahoe City is rich in historical significance, with a variety of sites and landmarks that tell the story of the area's past. In addition to its historical attractions, Tahoe City is also known for its scenic lakeside strolls, offering visitors the chance to enjoy the stunning beauty of Lake Tahoe in a relaxed and leisurely setting. Here's a guide to exploring the historic sites and lakeside strolls in Tahoe City.

HISTORIC SITES IN TAHOE CITY

Tahoe City's history dates back to the 19th century, and the town is home to several historic sites that provide a glimpse into the region's past. From museums and old cabins to iconic landmarks, these sites offer fascinating insights into the people and events that shaped the area.

1. GATEKEEPER'S MUSEUM AND THE MARION STEINBACH INDIAN BASKET MUSEUM

Overview:
The Gatekeeper's Museum is one of the most prominent historical sites in

Tahoe City. Located at the entrance to the Tahoe City Commons Beach, the museum is housed in a replica of the original gatekeeper's cabin, which was built in 1910. The museum focuses on the history of Tahoe City and the surrounding area, with exhibits that cover everything from the Washoe Tribe's native culture to the construction of the Lake Tahoe Dam.

Highlights:

- **Marion Steinbach Indian Basket Museum:** One of the most unique collections in the region, this museum within the Gatekeeper's Museum features an extensive array of Native American baskets, primarily from the Washoe Tribe. The baskets showcase intricate craftsmanship and are considered some of the finest examples of Native American art in the country.

- **Historic Exhibits:** The museum's exhibits explore various aspects of Tahoe City's history, including its role in the development of Lake Tahoe as a popular resort destination. Visitors can learn about the area's early settlers, the impact of the logging and railroad industries, and the evolution of the town over the years.

Why Visit: The Gatekeeper's Museum and the Marion Steinbach Indian Basket Museum offer a deep dive into the rich cultural heritage of Tahoe City and the Lake Tahoe region. It's a must-visit for history enthusiasts and anyone interested in learning more about the area's Native American history.

2. WATSON CABIN MUSEUM

Overview:
The Watson Cabin is the oldest structure in Tahoe City that's still in its original location. Built in 1909 by Robert Montgomery Watson, a prominent figure in the development of the area, the cabin has been preserved as a museum to showcase life in Tahoe City during the early 20th century. The cabin is listed on the National Register of Historic Places.

Highlights:

- **Historical Artifacts:** The cabin is filled with period furnishings and artifacts, giving visitors a sense of what life was like for the early residents of Tahoe City. The interior has been carefully restored to reflect the living conditions of the time.

- **Guided Tours:** The Watson Cabin Museum offers guided tours that provide detailed insights into the history of the cabin, the Watson family, and the early days of Tahoe City. The knowledgeable guides share fascinating stories about the challenges and triumphs of life in the Sierra Nevada mountains over a century ago.

Why Visit: The Watson Cabin Museum is a well-preserved example of early 20th-century architecture in Lake Tahoe and offers a unique window into the past. It's an excellent stop for those interested in the history of Tahoe City and the lifestyle of its early settlers.

3. LAKE TAHOE DAM AND FANNY BRIDGE

Overview:

The Lake Tahoe Dam, located at the headwaters of the Truckee River in Tahoe City, was completed in 1913 and plays a crucial role in regulating the water level of Lake Tahoe. The dam is an important piece of the area's history, as it transformed the lake into a major water storage reservoir. Just downstream from the dam is Fanny Bridge, a popular spot where visitors can watch fish swimming in the clear waters of the Truckee River.

Highlights:

- **Historic Engineering:** The Lake Tahoe Dam is a significant engineering feat of its time, and visitors can learn about its construction and its impact on the region. Informational plaques along the dam provide details about its history and operation.

- **Fanny Bridge:** Named for the sight of visitors leaning over to watch the fish (and thus showing their "fannies"), Fanny Bridge offers a charming view of the Truckee River and is a favorite spot for both locals and tourists. The bridge provides an up-close look at the river's aquatic life, including large trout that gather in the waters below.

Why Visit: The Lake Tahoe Dam and Fanny Bridge are key landmarks in Tahoe City that highlight the intersection of natural beauty and human ingenuity. The area around the dam is also a starting point for various lakeside strolls, making it an ideal spot to explore both history and nature.

4. TAHOE MARITIME MUSEUM

Overview:
Although the Tahoe Maritime Museum moved to Truckee in recent years, its legacy in Tahoe City is significant. The museum preserves and celebrates the maritime history of Lake Tahoe, focusing on the wooden boats that have plied the lake's waters for over a century. The collection includes historic vessels, maritime artifacts, and interactive exhibits.

Highlights:

- **Classic Wooden Boats:** The museum's collection includes beautifully restored wooden boats, some of which date back to the early 1900s. These boats are iconic symbols of Lake Tahoe's maritime history and are often featured in local boating events.

- **Maritime Artifacts:** The museum also houses a wide range of maritime artifacts, including navigational equipment, vintage photos, and ship models. These exhibits provide insight into the lake's boating culture and the evolution of watercraft over the years.

- **Educational Programs:** The Tahoe Maritime Museum offers educational programs and events throughout the year, including boat-building workshops, lectures, and guided tours. These programs are designed to engage visitors of all ages and deepen their understanding of the lake's maritime heritage.

Why Visit: Although now located in Truckee, the Tahoe Maritime Museum remains an important part of the Tahoe City cultural landscape. It's worth a visit for those interested in the history of boating on Lake Tahoe and the craftsmanship of classic wooden boats.

LAKESIDE STROLLS IN TAHOE CITY

In addition to its rich history, Tahoe City is also known for its scenic lakeside strolls, which offer visitors the opportunity to experience the natural beauty of Lake Tahoe up close. Whether you're looking for a leisurely walk along the shoreline or a more immersive exploration of the area's parks and trails, Tahoe City has plenty of options to choose from.

1. TAHOE CITY LAKESIDE TRAIL

Overview:
The Tahoe City Lakeside Trail, also known as the Tahoe City Bike Path, is a scenic multi-use trail that runs along the shoreline of Lake Tahoe. The trail stretches for several miles and offers stunning views of the lake, mountains, and surrounding forests. It's a popular spot for walking, jogging, biking, and picnicking.

Highlights:

- **Lakeside Views:** The trail offers continuous views of Lake Tahoe, with several spots where you can stop and take in the scenery. Benches and picnic tables are available along the route, providing perfect spots to relax and enjoy the view.

- **Easy Access:** The Tahoe City Lakeside Trail is easily accessible from several points in town, including the Tahoe City Commons Beach, making it a convenient option for a leisurely stroll.

- **Public Art and Historical Markers:** Along the trail, you'll find public art installations and historical markers that provide information about the area's history and natural environment. These add an educational element to the walk, making it both enjoyable and informative.

Why Walk Here: The Tahoe City Lakeside Trail is an easy and enjoyable way to experience the beauty of Lake Tahoe. Whether you're looking for a short walk or a longer stroll, this trail offers a relaxing way to connect with nature and take in the stunning views.

2. COMMONS BEACH PARK

Overview:
Commons Beach is one of Tahoe City's most popular public spaces, offering a wide sandy beach, picnic areas, and a large playground. The park is located right in the heart of town, making it a convenient spot for families and visitors looking to spend some time by the water.

Highlights:

- **Swimming and Sunbathing:** Commons Beach is a great spot for swimming and sunbathing during the summer months. The sandy beach is perfect for relaxing, and the shallow waters are ideal for wading and splashing.

- **Picnicking:** The park is equipped with picnic tables, BBQ grills, and plenty of grassy areas, making it a perfect place for a lakeside picnic. The views of Lake Tahoe from the picnic areas are spectacular, especially at sunset.

- **Sunday Concerts:** During the summer, Commons Beach hosts the Tahoe City Concerts at Commons Beach series, offering free live music performances every Sunday afternoon. These concerts are a local favorite and provide a festive atmosphere by the lake.

Why Visit: Commons Beach Park is a central gathering place in Tahoe City and offers a variety of activities for all ages. Whether you're enjoying a picnic, swimming in the lake, or attending a concert, Commons Beach is a must-visit spot for anyone exploring Tahoe City.

3. NORTH TAHOE REGIONAL PARK

Overview:

Located just a short drive from Tahoe City, North Tahoe Regional Park offers a more expansive setting for outdoor activities and lakeside strolls. The park features hiking and biking trails, sports fields, and picnic areas, all set against the backdrop of Lake Tahoe's natural beauty.

Highlights:

- **Hiking and Biking:** The park's trails wind through the forest and offer beautiful views of the lake and mountains. The trails vary in difficulty, making them suitable for both casual walkers and more experienced hikers.

- **Scenic Overlooks:** Several spots within the park offer panoramic views of Lake Tahoe, providing excellent opportunities for photography and sightseeing.

- **Winter Sports:** In the winter, the park is a popular spot for snowshoeing and cross-country skiing, with groomed trails and plenty of snow-covered terrain to explore.

Why Visit: orth Tahoe Regional Park is a great destination for those looking to immerse themselves in the natural beauty of Lake Tahoe. With its variety of trails and recreational opportunities, the park offers something for everyone, making it a perfect spot for a day of outdoor adventure.

4.4 NORTHSTAR CALIFORNIA: SKIING, BIKING, AND MORE

Northstar California Resort, nestled in the Sierra Nevada mountains near Lake Tahoe, is a premier destination for outdoor enthusiasts year-round. Whether you're drawn to the snow-covered slopes in the winter, the extensive mountain biking trails in the summer, or the luxury amenities and family-friendly activities, Northstar offers something for everyone. This guide will take you through the best of what Northstar California has to offer, from skiing and snowboarding in the winter to mountain biking and more during the warmer months.

WINTER ACTIVITIES AT NORTHSTAR CALIFORNIA

Northstar California is renowned for its world-class skiing and snowboarding, offering a variety of terrain that caters to all levels, from beginners to advanced riders. The resort is also known for its family-friendly atmosphere, excellent ski schools, and luxurious amenities, making it a top choice for winter getaways.

1. SKIING AND SNOWBOARDING

Overview:
Northstar features over 3,000 acres of skiable terrain, with 100 runs serviced by 20 lifts, including high-speed quads and gondolas. The resort is known for its impeccably groomed trails, scenic glades, and challenging terrain parks, making it a favorite among skiers and snowboarders alike.

Terrain for All Levels:

- **Beginners:** Northstar is an excellent resort for beginners, with a dedicated learning area at the base of the mountain and a variety of gentle green runs perfect for those just starting out.

- **Intermediates:** Intermediate skiers and snowboarders will find plenty of blue runs to explore, with wide, groomed trails that offer a comfortable yet exciting experience.

- **Advanced:** For those seeking a challenge, Northstar offers advanced terrain with black diamond runs, steep moguls, and tree skiing. The Backside and Lookout Mountain areas are known for their more difficult runs, providing thrilling experiences for expert skiers and riders.

Terrain Parks: Northstar is also home to some of the best terrain parks in the Lake Tahoe area, catering to all skill levels:

- **The Straits:** A top-notch park for advanced riders, featuring large jumps, rails, and other challenging features.

- **The Stash:** A unique park with natural features like logs, stumps, and wooden rails, designed in collaboration with Burton Snowboards.

- **Pinball:** A beginner-friendly terrain park that offers smaller jumps and features, perfect for those new to freestyle riding.

Night Skiing: For those who can't get enough of the slopes, Northstar offers night skiing on select trails, providing a unique and thrilling experience under the stars.

2. CROSS-COUNTRY SKIING AND SNOWSHOEING

Overview:
In addition to downhill skiing and snowboarding, Northstar offers cross-country skiing and snowshoeing trails that wind through the beautiful Sierra Nevada landscape. The resort's cross-country center provides access to over 35 kilometers of groomed trails suitable for both classic and skate skiing, as well as snowshoeing.

Why Try It:

- **Peaceful Scenery:** Cross-country skiing and snowshoeing allow you to explore the quieter, more serene parts of the mountain, with opportunities to see wildlife and take in the stunning winter scenery.

- **Fitness:** Both activities provide an excellent workout, combining cardiovascular exercise with the beauty of nature.

Rentals and Lessons: The cross-country center offers equipment rentals, lessons, and guided tours, making it easy for beginners to get started and for more experienced skiers to improve their technique.

3. ICE SKATING

Overview:

The ice skating rink at Northstar's Village is a popular spot for families and couples looking to enjoy a classic winter activity. The rink is open daily during the winter season and is surrounded by cozy fire pits, where you can warm up with a hot chocolate or a glass of wine.

Highlights:

- **Festive Atmosphere:** The rink is the heart of the Village at Northstar, offering a festive and lively atmosphere with twinkling lights, music, and plenty of seating for spectators.

- **Family-Friendly:** Ice skating at Northstar is perfect for families, with skate rentals available on-site and plenty of nearby dining options for post-skating meals.

4. Après-Ski and Dining

Overview:

Northstar is known for its vibrant après-ski scene, with a variety of bars, lounges, and restaurants where you can relax after a day on the slopes.

Top Spots:

- **The Village at Northstar:** The Village is the center of activity, offering a range of dining options from casual eateries to fine dining. Popular spots include **TC's Pub** for hearty fare and craft beers, and **Rubicon Pizza Company** for family-friendly dining.

- **Ritz-Carlton Lake Tahoe:** For a more upscale après-ski experience, head to the Ritz-Carlton, located mid-mountain. The **Highlands Bar** offers gourmet appetizers, signature cocktails, and stunning views of the surrounding mountains.

- **Live Music and Fire Pits:** The Village often hosts live music events, and the outdoor fire pits provide a cozy spot to unwind with friends or family.

SUMMER ACTIVITIES AT NORTHSTAR CALIFORNIA

When the snow melts, Northstar transforms into a summer paradise, offering a wide range of activities for outdoor enthusiasts. From mountain biking to hiking and more, the resort provides plenty of opportunities to explore the beauty of the Sierra Nevada during the warmer months.

1. MOUNTAIN BIKING

Overview:
Northstar is a premier destination for mountain biking, featuring over 100 miles of trails that cater to all levels, from beginners to expert riders. The resort's bike park is known for its well-maintained trails, challenging downhill runs, and scenic cross-country routes.

Trail Highlights:

- **Beginner Trails:** For those new to mountain biking, Northstar offers a variety of beginner-friendly trails with gentle descents and wide paths. **Easy Rider** and **Coaster** are great options for first-timers.

- **Intermediate Trails:** Intermediate riders will enjoy trails like **Livewire**, Northstar's signature flow trail, which features smooth berms, jumps, and rollers.

- **Advanced Trails:** For expert riders, Northstar's advanced trails offer steep descents, technical rock gardens, and challenging jumps. Trails like **Boondocks** and **Gypsy** are perfect for those seeking a thrill.

Bike Rentals and Lessons: Northstar's bike park offers bike rentals, including full-suspension mountain bikes and protective gear. The resort also provides lessons and guided tours, making it easy for beginners to get started and for experienced riders to tackle more challenging terrain.

2. HIKING

Overview:

Northstar offers a variety of hiking trails that wind through the scenic Sierra Nevada, providing stunning views of Lake Tahoe and the surrounding mountains. Whether you're looking for a leisurely walk or a more challenging hike, there's a trail for everyone.

Trail Highlights:

- **Sawmill Lake Trail:** This moderate hike is a 2.3-mile round trip that leads to a beautiful alpine lake. The trail offers scenic views and is perfect for families and casual hikers.

- **Martis Valley Loop:** A longer, more challenging hike, the Martis Valley Loop is a 9-mile trail that offers panoramic views of Martis Valley and Lake Tahoe. The trail is known for its wildflower displays in the summer and provides a peaceful escape into nature.

- **Tahoe Rim Trail:** Northstar provides access to portions of the Tahoe Rim Trail, a renowned 165-mile trail that circles Lake Tahoe. Hiking sections of this trail offers breathtaking views and a more rugged hiking experience.

Guided Hikes: Northstar offers guided hikes led by knowledgeable guides who provide insights into the area's flora, fauna, and history. These hikes are a great way to learn more about the natural environment while enjoying the beauty of the mountains.

3. GOLFING AT NORTHSTAR CALIFORNIA

Overview:

Northstar features an 18-hole championship golf course designed by Robert Muir Graves, offering a challenging and scenic experience for golfers of all levels. The course is set amidst the stunning alpine landscape, with fairways lined by towering pines and beautiful views of the surrounding mountains.

Course Features:

- **18-Hole Course:** The par-72 course features a mix of long, open fairways and more challenging, tree-lined holes, providing a varied and enjoyable round of golf.

- **Practice Facilities:** The course offers a driving range, putting green, and chipping area, allowing golfers to warm up and practice their skills before hitting the course.

- **Clubhouse:** The Northstar Golf Course clubhouse offers a pro shop, where you can purchase golf gear and apparel, as well as a restaurant and bar with outdoor seating overlooking the course.

Why Play Here: Golfing at Northstar provides a unique opportunity to enjoy a round of golf in one of the most beautiful settings in Lake Tahoe. The combination of challenging play and breathtaking scenery makes it a must-visit for any golf enthusiast.

4. KID-FRIENDLY ACTIVITIES

Overview:
Northstar is a family-friendly resort, offering a variety of activities for kids and families during the summer months. From adventure camps to outdoor games, there's plenty to keep the little ones entertained.

Top Activities:

- **Kids Adventure Camp:** Northstar offers summer adventure camps for kids, featuring activities like rock climbing, zip-lining, arts and crafts, and nature hikes. The camps are designed to provide a fun and educational outdoor experience for children.

- **Miniature Golf:** The resort's Village features a fun and challenging miniature golf course that's perfect for families. The course is themed around Lake Tahoe's history and natural environment, adding an educational element to the fun.

- **Gem Panning:** Kids can try their hand at gem panning in the Village, where they can search for hidden treasures in a replica mining sluice. It's a fun and interactive way to learn about the region's mining history.

5. SCENIC CHAIRLIFT RIDES

Overview:
In the summer, Northstar offers scenic chairlift rides that provide breathtaking views of Lake Tahoe and the surrounding mountains. The chairlifts take you up the mountain, where you can enjoy the panoramic vistas or start a hike from one of the upper trails.

Why Try It:

- **Stunning Views:** The chairlift rides offer some of the best views in the region, with Lake Tahoe and the Sierra Nevada mountains providing a stunning backdrop.

- **Relaxing Experience:** The rides are a relaxing way to take in the beauty of the area without the exertion of hiking. It's a perfect activity for those looking to enjoy the scenery in comfort.

CHAPTER 5: OUTDOOR ACTIVITIES IN LAKE TAHOE

5.1 HIKING TRAILS: FROM EASY WALKS TO CHALLENGING TREKS

If you're looking for a relaxing and accessible way to enjoy the beauty of Lake Tahoe, these easy walks offer breathtaking scenery with minimal elevation gain. Perfect for families, beginners, or anyone seeking a peaceful day in nature, these trails provide an opportunity to connect with the stunning landscapes of the region without the intensity of a more challenging hike.

1. EAGLE ROCK TRAIL

Location: West Shore, near Homewood
Distance: 1.5 miles round trip
Elevation Gain: 250 feet
Difficulty: Easy

Overview:
Eagle Rock Trail is a short, easy hike that offers some of the best panoramic views of Lake Tahoe from the top of Eagle Rock, a volcanic outcrop on the lake's western shore. The trail is well-maintained and accessible, making it a popular choice for families and casual hikers.

Highlights:

- **Scenic Overlook:** The summit of Eagle Rock provides a stunning view of the lake, with the azure waters framed by the surrounding mountains. It's a perfect spot for photography or a picnic.

- **Quick and Accessible:** The trail is short and relatively easy, making it a great option for those with limited time or for a quick outing.

2. TAHOE MEADOWS INTERPRETIVE LOOP

Location: North Shore, near Incline Village
Distance: 1.3 miles round trip
Elevation Gain: 50 feet
Difficulty: Easy

Overview:
The Tahoe Meadows Interpretive Loop is a gentle, family-friendly hike that takes you through a beautiful alpine meadow on the north shore of Lake Tahoe. The trail is mostly flat, with well-maintained paths and interpretive signs that provide information about the local flora and fauna.

Highlights:

- **Alpine Meadow:** The trail winds through a lush meadow filled with wildflowers in the spring and summer, offering a serene and picturesque setting.

- **Educational Experience:** The interpretive signs along the trail make this hike both enjoyable and informative, providing insights into the natural environment of the Lake Tahoe area.

3. RUBICON TRAIL (LAKESIDE SECTION)

Location: West Shore, between D.L. Bliss State Park and Emerald Bay
Distance: 3 miles round trip (D.L. Bliss to Emerald Bay)
Elevation Gain: 100 feet
Difficulty: Easy

Overview:
The Rubicon Trail is one of the most scenic and popular hikes in Lake Tahoe, and the lakeside section between D.L. Bliss State Park and Emerald Bay offers an easy, yet stunning, walk along the shoreline. The trail hugs the water's edge, providing continuous views of the lake and the surrounding mountains.

Highlights:

- **Lakeside Views:** This section of the Rubicon Trail offers uninterrupted views of Lake Tahoe's clear blue waters, with several spots where you can stop to dip your feet or enjoy a picnic.

- **Emerald Bay:** The trail leads to Emerald Bay, one of the most iconic and photographed spots in Lake Tahoe, known for its striking emerald-green waters and Fannette Island.

MODERATE HIKES: SCENIC TRAILS WITH A BIT OF CHALLENGE

For those looking to explore more of Lake Tahoe's diverse landscapes, these moderate hikes offer a rewarding mix of scenic views, varied terrain, and a bit more physical challenge. These trails are ideal for hikers with some experience who are looking to spend a few hours immersed in nature.

4. MOUNT TALLAC TRAIL

Location: South Shore, near South Lake Tahoe
Distance: 10 miles round trip
Elevation Gain: 3,300 feet
Difficulty: Moderate to Strenuous

Overview:
Mount Tallac is one of the most popular hikes in the Lake Tahoe area, offering incredible views of the lake and the surrounding wilderness. While the trail is long and has a significant elevation gain, the rewards at the summit are well worth the effort.

Highlights:

- **Summit Views:** The summit of Mount Tallac provides breathtaking, panoramic views of Lake Tahoe, Desolation Wilderness, and the Sierra Nevada mountains. On a clear day, you can see for miles in every direction.

- **Wildflowers and Lakes:** Along the way, hikers pass through alpine meadows, past small mountain lakes, and through fields of wildflowers, making the journey as beautiful as the destination.

5. EAGLE LAKE TRAIL

Location: West Shore, near Emerald Bay
Distance: 2 miles round trip
Elevation Gain: 400 feet
Difficulty: Moderate

Overview:
Eagle Lake Trail is a short but rewarding hike that takes you from the shores of Emerald Bay up to the serene Eagle Lake, nestled in the mountains. The trail offers a moderate challenge with a steady climb, but the distance is manageable for most hikers.

Highlights:

- **Eagle Falls:** The trail begins near the beautiful Eagle Falls, a popular spot for photography and a great place to start your hike.

- **Eagle Lake:** The destination, Eagle Lake, is a tranquil alpine lake surrounded by granite peaks. It's a perfect spot for a picnic, swimming, or simply enjoying the natural beauty.

6. CASCADE FALLS TRAIL

Location: West Shore, near Emerald Bay
Distance: 1.5 miles round trip
Elevation Gain: 500 feet
Difficulty: Moderate

Overview:
The Cascade Falls Trail is a relatively short hike that offers stunning views of Cascade Lake and Lake Tahoe. The trail leads to the picturesque Cascade Falls, which tumbles down granite cliffs into the lake below. The hike is moderately challenging, with some rocky sections and a gradual climb.

Highlights:

- **Cascade Falls:** The main attraction of this hike is the beautiful Cascade Falls, which flows year-round and is especially impressive in the spring when the snowmelt is at its peak.

- **Panoramic Views:** Along the trail, you'll enjoy stunning views of both Cascade Lake and Lake Tahoe, making it a great hike for photographers and nature lovers.

7. FALLEN LEAF LAKE TRAIL

Location: South Shore, near South Lake Tahoe
Distance: 8 miles round trip
Elevation Gain: 200 feet
Difficulty: Moderate

Overview:
Fallen Leaf Lake Trail is a peaceful hike that takes you around the shores of Fallen Leaf Lake, a smaller and quieter alternative to Lake Tahoe. The trail is relatively flat but long, making it a moderate challenge that's perfect for a full day of hiking.

Highlights:

- **Lake Views:** The trail offers continuous views of Fallen Leaf Lake, with several spots where you can stop to swim, fish, or just relax by the water.

- **Wildlife:** The area around Fallen Leaf Lake is home to a variety of wildlife, including deer, birds, and the occasional black bear, making it a great spot for wildlife watching.

CHALLENGING TREKS: RUGGED ADVENTURES FOR THE EXPERIENCED HIKER

For those seeking a true adventure and a physical challenge, these difficult hikes offer rugged terrain, significant elevation gains, and some of the most rewarding views in the Lake Tahoe area. These treks are best suited for experienced hikers who are prepared for a full day on the trail.

8. MOUNT ROSE TRAIL

Location: North Shore, near Incline Village
Distance: 10.5 miles round trip
Elevation Gain: 2,500 feet
Difficulty: Strenuous

Overview:
Mount Rose is the third-highest peak in the Lake Tahoe basin, and the trail to the summit offers a challenging hike with incredible rewards. The trail is long and steep, but the panoramic views from the top are some of the best in the region.

Highlights:

- **Summit Views:** From the summit of Mount Rose, you can see all of Lake Tahoe, the Carson Range, and the Nevada desert. It's a breathtaking 360-degree view that's worth the effort.

- **Wildflowers:** In the summer, the lower sections of the trail are lined with wildflowers, adding a splash of color to the rugged landscape.

9. FREEL PEAK TRAIL

Location: South Shore, near South Lake Tahoe
Distance: 11 miles round trip
Elevation Gain: 3,200 feet
Difficulty: Strenuous

Overview:
Freel Peak is the highest point in the Lake Tahoe basin, standing at 10,886 feet. The trail to the summit is long, steep, and challenging, but the views from the top are unmatched. This hike is a true test of endurance and is best suited for experienced hikers.

Highlights:

- **Highest Point:** Reaching the summit of Freel Peak is a significant achievement, offering unparalleled views of Lake Tahoe, the Carson Valley, and the Sierra Nevada mountains.

- **Remote Wilderness:** The trail passes through remote and pristine wilderness areas, providing a sense of solitude and adventure.

10. DESOLATION WILDERNESS - PACIFIC CREST TRAIL (ECHO LAKES TO ALOHA LAKE)

Location: West Shore, near Echo Lake
Distance: 12 miles round trip

Elevation Gain: 1,800 feet
Difficulty: Strenuous

Overview:
This section of the Pacific Crest Trail takes you through the heart of Desolation Wilderness, one of the most rugged and beautiful areas in the Lake Tahoe region. The trail starts at Echo Lakes and leads to Aloha Lake, passing through granite landscapes, alpine lakes, and high mountain passes.

Highlights:

- **Desolation Wilderness:** The Desolation Wilderness is a protected area known for its dramatic granite peaks, crystal-clear lakes, and remote wilderness feel. It's a paradise for hikers seeking solitude and natural beauty.

- **Aloha Lake:** The destination, Aloha Lake, is a stunning alpine lake surrounded by rocky peaks. The lake is dotted with small islands and is a perfect spot for a rest or a swim after a challenging hike.

5.2 WATER SPORTS: BOATING, KAYAKING, AND PADDLEBOARDING

Lake Tahoe, with its crystal-clear waters and stunning alpine surroundings, is a paradise for water sports enthusiasts. Whether you're looking to explore the lake's serene coves by kayak, glide across the water on a paddleboard, or enjoy the thrill of boating, Lake Tahoe offers a wide range of activities for all skill levels. Here's a comprehensive guide to the best water sports experiences on Lake Tahoe, including boating, kayaking, and paddleboarding.

BOATING ON LAKE TAHOE

Boating is one of the most popular activities on Lake Tahoe, offering a thrilling way to experience the lake's vastness and natural beauty. With over 70 miles of shoreline and numerous marinas, Lake Tahoe provides ample opportunities for boating enthusiasts to explore its deep blue waters.

1. RENTING A BOAT

Overview:
Boat rentals are available at several marinas around Lake Tahoe, making it easy for visitors to get out on the water. Whether you're looking for a speedboat, a pontoon boat for a relaxing day with family, or a luxury yacht for a special occasion, there's a boat rental option to suit every need.

Top Marinas for Rentals:

- **Tahoe Keys Marina (South Lake Tahoe):** One of the largest marinas on the lake, Tahoe Keys Marina offers a wide range of boats for rent, including speedboats, pontoons, and fishing boats. The marina also provides amenities like fuel, bait, and supplies, making it a convenient starting point for a day on the water.

- **Ski Run Marina (South Lake Tahoe):** Located near the Heavenly Village, Ski Run Marina offers boat rentals, water sports equipment, and even parasailing adventures. It's a great option for those staying in South Lake Tahoe.

- **North Tahoe Marina (Tahoe Vista):** This marina on the North Shore offers a variety of boats for rent, from luxury pontoons to fishing boats. They also provide boat launching and fueling services.

Why Rent a Boat:

- **Explore the Lake:** Renting a boat allows you to explore Lake Tahoe at your own pace, visiting secluded coves, beaches, and even Fannette Island in Emerald Bay.

- **Water Sports:** Many boat rental companies offer additional equipment like wakeboards, water skis, and inner tubes, making it easy to enjoy a variety of water sports.

2. BOATING TOURS AND CRUISES

Overview:
For those who prefer a guided experience, Lake Tahoe offers a variety of boating tours and cruises that showcase the lake's most beautiful spots. From sunset cruises to historical tours, these boat trips provide a relaxing and informative way to enjoy Lake Tahoe.

Popular Tours:

- **M.S. Dixie II Paddlewheeler (Zephyr Cove):** The M.S. Dixie II is a classic paddlewheel boat that offers daily cruises on Lake Tahoe, including scenic tours of Emerald Bay and sunset dinner cruises. The narrated tours provide insights into the lake's history, geology, and ecology.

- **Tahoe Gal (Tahoe City):** The Tahoe Gal offers a range of cruises departing from Tahoe City Marina, including lunch and dinner cruises, as well as private charters. The boat's comfortable seating and open decks provide excellent views of the lake and surrounding mountains.

Why Take a Tour:

- **Relax and Learn:** Boating tours offer a relaxing way to experience Lake Tahoe while learning about the area's natural and cultural history from knowledgeable guides.

- **Scenic Views:** The cruises provide some of the best views of Lake Tahoe's shoreline, including iconic spots like Emerald Bay and the historic Vikingsholm mansion.

3. FISHING ON LAKE TAHOE

Overview:
Lake Tahoe is a popular destination for fishing, offering opportunities to catch species like Mackinaw (Lake Trout), Rainbow Trout, Brown Trout,

and Kokanee Salmon. Whether you're an experienced angler or a beginner, fishing on Lake Tahoe is a rewarding experience.

Fishing Options:

- **Charter Fishing:** Several companies offer guided fishing charters on Lake Tahoe, providing all the equipment and expertise needed for a successful day on the water. These charters often focus on deep-water fishing for Mackinaw, which can grow to impressive sizes in the lake's depths.

- **Shore Fishing:** For those who prefer to stay on land, shore fishing is also popular in certain areas of Lake Tahoe, especially near river inlets and rocky points. Kings Beach, Tahoe Keys, and Sand Harbor are all good spots to try your luck.

Why Go Fishing:

- **Catch Your Dinner:** Lake Tahoe's clear waters are home to a variety of fish species, making it a great place to catch fresh, delicious fish for dinner.

- **Peaceful Experience:** Fishing on Lake Tahoe offers a peaceful and meditative experience, with the stunning backdrop of the Sierra Nevada mountains enhancing the tranquility.

KAYAKING ON LAKE TAHOE

Kayaking is one of the best ways to explore Lake Tahoe's shoreline and get up close to its natural beauty. With its calm waters and numerous secluded coves, Lake Tahoe is a kayaker's dream, offering both serene paddling experiences and more challenging routes for adventurous paddlers.

1. KAYAK RENTALS AND GUIDED TOURS

Overview:
Kayak rentals are widely available around Lake Tahoe, with options ranging from single kayaks to tandem models for two people. Guided tours are also

available for those who want to learn more about the lake's history, geology, and ecology while exploring its waters.

Top Rental Locations:

- **Tahoe City Kayak (Tahoe City):** Located on the North Shore, Tahoe City Kayak offers a variety of kayaks for rent, as well as guided tours that explore the scenic shoreline of Lake Tahoe.

- **Kayak Tahoe (Multiple Locations):** With rental locations in South Lake Tahoe, Emerald Bay, and Sand Harbor, Kayak Tahoe is a convenient option for those looking to explore different parts of the lake.

Popular Guided Tours:

- **Emerald Bay Kayak Tour:** This guided tour takes paddlers into the heart of Emerald Bay, one of the most beautiful and iconic spots on Lake Tahoe. The tour includes stops at Fannette Island and the historic Vikingsholm mansion, providing both adventure and historical insights.

- **Sunset Kayak Tour:** Experience the magic of a Lake Tahoe sunset from the water with a guided sunset kayak tour. These tours typically depart in the evening and offer stunning views of the sun setting over the Sierra Nevada mountains.

Why Kayak:

- **Explore Hidden Coves:** Kayaking allows you to reach secluded beaches and coves that are inaccessible by larger boats, giving you a more intimate experience of Lake Tahoe's natural beauty.

- **Exercise and Adventure:** Paddling a kayak provides a great workout while also offering the thrill of exploring Lake Tahoe at your own pace.

2. TOP KAYAKING SPOTS

Overview:

Lake Tahoe offers a variety of kayaking spots, each with its own unique charm and scenic beauty. Whether you're looking for a calm paddle along the shoreline or an adventurous journey to a remote island, these top kayaking spots in Lake Tahoe have something to offer.

Best Spots for Kayaking:

- **Emerald Bay:** Emerald Bay is one of the most popular kayaking destinations on Lake Tahoe, known for its emerald-green waters and the stunning Fannette Island. The sheltered bay provides calm waters for paddling and plenty of opportunities for exploration.

- **Sand Harbor:** Located on the Nevada side of the lake, Sand Harbor is a favorite spot for kayakers due to its crystal-clear waters and scenic rock formations. The sandy beaches and shallow waters make it a perfect place for a relaxing paddle.

- **D.L. Bliss State Park:** This park on the West Shore offers excellent kayaking opportunities, with beautiful views of the granite cliffs and the deep blue waters of Lake Tahoe. The calm waters near the shore make it a great spot for beginners.

Why Kayak Here:

- **Scenic Beauty:** These kayaking spots are known for their stunning scenery, from the towering cliffs of Emerald Bay to the clear waters and sandy beaches of Sand Harbor.

- **Wildlife Viewing:** Kayaking offers a unique perspective for spotting wildlife, including fish, birds, and even the occasional bear near the shoreline.

PADDLEBOARDING ON LAKE TAHOE

Paddleboarding has become one of the most popular water sports on Lake Tahoe, offering a fun and accessible way to enjoy the lake's calm waters. Whether you're a beginner or an experienced paddler, Lake Tahoe's clear waters and stunning scenery make it an ideal destination for paddleboarding.

1. PADDLEBOARD RENTALS AND LESSONS

Overview:
Paddleboard rentals are available at many locations around Lake Tahoe, and lessons are often offered for beginners who want to learn the basics of balance and paddling. Renting a paddleboard is an easy way to get out on the water and experience the tranquility of Lake Tahoe.

Top Rental Locations:

- **South Tahoe Standup Paddle (South Lake Tahoe):** This rental shop offers a variety of paddleboards, including all-around boards for beginners and performance boards for more experienced paddlers. They also offer lessons and guided tours.

- **Waterman's Landing (Carnelian Bay):** Located on the North Shore, Waterman's Landing is a popular spot for paddleboard rentals and lessons. The calm waters of Carnelian Bay make it a perfect place for paddleboarding, especially for beginners.

Why Rent a Paddleboard:

- **Explore at Your Own Pace:** Paddleboarding allows you to explore the lake at a leisurely pace, taking in the scenery and enjoying the peaceful surroundings.

- **Fitness Benefits:** Paddleboarding provides a full-body workout, helping to improve balance, strength, and endurance while enjoying the beauty of Lake Tahoe.

2. TOP PADDLEBOARDING SPOTS

Overview:
Lake Tahoe offers a variety of great spots for paddleboarding, each with its own unique features and scenic views. Whether you're looking for calm

waters for a relaxing paddle or more open water for a challenging workout, these spots are perfect for paddleboarding.

Best Spots for Paddleboarding:

- **Sand Harbor:** Sand Harbor is one of the most popular paddleboarding spots on Lake Tahoe, known for its clear, shallow waters and stunning rock formations. The sandy beaches and calm waters make it an ideal location for beginners and experienced paddlers alike.

- **Kings Beach:** Located on the North Shore, Kings Beach offers a large, sandy beach and calm waters perfect for paddleboarding. The expansive shoreline provides plenty of space to explore, and the nearby amenities make it a convenient spot for a day on the water.

- **Tahoe City Commons Beach:** This centrally located beach on the North Shore is a great spot for paddleboarding, with easy access to rentals and plenty of space to paddle along the shoreline. The views of the surrounding mountains and the open waters of Lake Tahoe make it a favorite among paddleboarders.

Why Paddleboard Here:

- **Crystal-Clear Waters:** The waters of Lake Tahoe are known for their clarity, allowing you to see the lakebed even in deeper areas. This makes paddleboarding on Lake Tahoe a visually stunning experience.

- **Peaceful Environment:** Paddleboarding offers a quiet and peaceful way to enjoy the beauty of Lake Tahoe, allowing you to connect with nature and escape the hustle and bustle of daily life.

5.3 CAMPING AND RVING: THE BEST SPOTS AROUND THE LAKE

Whether you're looking to pitch a tent under the stars, park your RV with full amenities, or enjoy a lakeside camping experience, Lake Tahoe has something to offer for everyone. Here's a guide to the best spots around Lake Tahoe for camping and RVing.

1. D.L. BLISS STATE PARK CAMPGROUND

Location: West Shore, near Emerald Bay

Overview:
D.L. Bliss State Park is one of the most popular camping spots on Lake Tahoe's West Shore, known for its stunning scenery and excellent access to outdoor activities. The campground is nestled among towering pines and offers easy access to the beach, hiking trails, and some of the most picturesque views of the lake.

Highlights:

- **Beach Access:** The park's beautiful sandy beach, Lester Beach, is just a short walk from the campground. It's a perfect spot for swimming, kayaking, and sunbathing.

- **Hiking Trails:** The campground is close to the Rubicon Trail, one of the most scenic hiking trails in Lake Tahoe, which offers breathtaking views of the lake and the surrounding mountains.

- **Campground Features:** The campground offers 165 sites for tents and RVs, with amenities including picnic tables, fire rings, restrooms, and hot showers. Some sites offer partial lake views.

Why Camp Here: D.L. Bliss State Park is ideal for those looking for a classic Lake Tahoe camping experience with easy access to the water and some of the best hiking trails in the area. The combination of natural beauty and well-maintained facilities makes it a favorite among campers.

2. FALLEN LEAF CAMPGROUND

Location: South Shore, near Fallen Leaf Lake

Overview:
Fallen Leaf Campground is located near the southern tip of Lake Tahoe, just a short distance from the beautiful Fallen Leaf Lake. This peaceful campground offers a more secluded experience, with access to both Fallen Leaf Lake and Lake Tahoe, making it a perfect spot for those who want to enjoy the tranquility of nature.

Highlights:

- **Fallen Leaf Lake:** The campground is just a short walk from the shores of Fallen Leaf Lake, a smaller and quieter alternative to Lake Tahoe. The lake is great for fishing, kayaking, and canoeing.

- **Hiking and Biking:** The campground is close to several hiking and biking trails, including the scenic Glen Alpine Trail and the Moraine Trail, which offers views of both Fallen Leaf Lake and Lake Tahoe.

- **Campground Features:** Fallen Leaf Campground offers 206 sites for tents, RVs, and trailers, with amenities including restrooms, hot showers, and a general store. Some sites offer views of the lake, and there are also group sites available.

Why Camp Here: Fallen Leaf Campground is perfect for those looking for a more secluded camping experience with easy access to both lakes. The campground's serene setting and proximity to hiking trails make it an excellent choice for nature lovers and outdoor enthusiasts.

3. MEEKS BAY RESORT AND MARINA

Location: West Shore, near Meeks Bay

Overview:
Meeks Bay Resort and Marina is a popular camping destination on the West Shore of Lake Tahoe, known for its beautiful sandy beach and clear waters. The resort offers a variety of accommodations, including campsites, cabins, and RV sites, making it a versatile option for families and groups.

Highlights:

- **Beach Access:** The resort's sandy beach is one of the best in Lake Tahoe, offering safe and shallow waters perfect for swimming, kayaking, and paddleboarding. The beach is also a great spot for relaxing and taking in the views of the lake.

- **Marina:** The resort's marina offers boat rentals, including kayaks, paddleboards, and motorboats, making it easy to explore Lake Tahoe by water.

- **Campground Features:** Meeks Bay Resort offers campsites for tents and RVs, as well as cabins for those looking for a more comfortable stay. The campground includes amenities such as restrooms, showers, and picnic areas.

Why Camp Here: Meeks Bay Resort is ideal for families and groups looking for a full-service camping experience with easy access to the beach and water activities. The resort's amenities and beautiful setting make it a popular choice for a fun and relaxing Lake Tahoe getaway.

4. CAMP RICHARDSON HISTORIC RESORT AND MARINA

Location: South Shore, near South Lake Tahoe

Overview:
Camp Richardson Historic Resort and Marina is a year-round destination that offers a variety of lodging options, including tent camping, RV sites, cabins, and hotel rooms. Located on the southern shore of Lake Tahoe, the resort is known for its historic charm, beautiful scenery, and extensive recreational activities.

Highlights:

- **Historic Charm:** Camp Richardson has a rich history dating back to the 1920s, and the resort maintains its vintage charm with rustic cabins and historic buildings. The resort's ice cream parlor and general store add to the nostalgic feel.

- **Recreational Activities:** The resort offers a wide range of activities, including biking, hiking, horseback riding, and water sports. The marina provides rentals for boats, kayaks, and paddleboards, and the resort's beach is perfect for swimming and relaxing.

- **Campground Features:** Camp Richardson offers a mix of tent sites, RV sites with full hookups, and cabins. The campground includes amenities such as restrooms, showers, and picnic areas.

Why Camp Here: Camp Richardson is perfect for those looking for a mix of outdoor adventure and historic charm. The resort's wide range of activities and accommodations make it an ideal destination for families and groups, as well as anyone looking to experience the best of Lake Tahoe's South Shore.

5. TAHOE VALLEY CAMPGROUND

Location: South Shore, near South Lake Tahoe

Overview:
Tahoe Valley Campground is a large, full-service RV park and campground located in South Lake Tahoe. With its spacious sites, modern amenities, and convenient location, Tahoe Valley Campground is a great choice for RVers and campers looking to enjoy the Lake Tahoe area.

Highlights:

- **Full Hookups:** The campground offers full hookups for RVs, including water, sewer, and electricity, making it a convenient option for those traveling with larger RVs or trailers.

- **Recreational Facilities:** Tahoe Valley Campground offers a variety of on-site recreational facilities, including a swimming pool, tennis courts, basketball courts, and a playground. The campground also organizes activities and events for guests.

- **Proximity to South Lake Tahoe:** The campground is just a short drive from the attractions and amenities of South Lake Tahoe, including restaurants, shops, and casinos. It's also close to popular outdoor activities like hiking, biking, and water sports.

Why Camp Here: Tahoe Valley Campground is ideal for RVers and campers looking for a full-service campground with modern amenities and easy access to South Lake Tahoe. The campground's facilities and convenient location make it a great base for exploring the area.

6. NEVADA BEACH CAMPGROUND

Location: East Shore, near Zephyr Cove

Overview:
Nevada Beach Campground is a beautiful lakeside campground located on the eastern shore of Lake Tahoe, near Zephyr Cove. The campground is known for its stunning beachfront location, offering easy access to the lake and breathtaking views of the surrounding mountains.

Highlights:

- **Lakeside Camping:** Nevada Beach Campground offers some of the best lakeside camping in Lake Tahoe, with campsites just steps away from the water. The sandy beach is perfect for swimming, sunbathing, and picnicking.

- **Scenic Views:** The campground offers panoramic views of Lake Tahoe and the Sierra Nevada mountains, making it a perfect spot for watching sunsets and stargazing.

- **Campground Features:** Nevada Beach Campground offers 54 sites for tents and RVs, with amenities including restrooms, picnic tables, fire rings, and drinking water. The campground also has a group site available for larger gatherings.

Why Camp Here: Nevada Beach Campground is perfect for those looking for a peaceful lakeside camping experience with easy access to the water.

The campground's scenic location and beautiful beach make it a favorite among campers who want to enjoy the natural beauty of Lake Tahoe.

7. ZEPHYR COVE RESORT AND CAMPGROUND

Location: East Shore, near Zephyr Cove

Overview:
Zephyr Cove Resort and Campground is a popular destination on the eastern shore of Lake Tahoe, offering a wide range of accommodations, including tent sites, RV sites, and cabins. The resort is known for its beautiful beach, marina, and variety of recreational activities.

Highlights:

- **Beach and Marina:** Zephyr Cove's sandy beach is one of the most popular on Lake Tahoe, offering plenty of space for swimming, sunbathing, and water sports. The marina provides rentals for boats, jet skis, kayaks, and paddleboards, making it easy to explore the lake.

- **Recreational Activities:** The resort offers a variety of activities, including horseback riding, boat cruises, and parasailing. The resort's restaurant and beachside bar are perfect for relaxing after a day of adventure.

- **Campground Features:** Zephyr Cove Campground offers sites for tents and RVs, with amenities including full hookups, restrooms, showers, and laundry facilities. The campground also has cabins available for those seeking a more comfortable stay.

Why Camp Here: Zephyr Cove Resort and Campground is ideal for those looking for a lively and active camping experience with plenty of amenities and activities. The resort's beach and marina make it a perfect destination for water sports enthusiasts, and the variety of accommodations makes it suitable for all types of campers.

5.4 Fishing and Wildlife Viewing: Connecting with Nature

1. Lake Tahoe's Fish Species Lake Tahoe is home to a variety of fish species, making it a prime location for anglers of all skill levels. The lake's cold, clear waters are ideal for species like Mackinaw (Lake Trout), Rainbow Trout, Brown Trout, and Kokanee Salmon. The experience of reeling in one of these prized catches is enhanced by the stunning backdrop of the Sierra Nevada mountains, creating a perfect blend of relaxation and excitement.

2. Popular Fishing Spots Some of the best fishing spots in Lake Tahoe include the deep waters of the north shore, where Mackinaw trout thrive, and the shallow areas near Sand Harbor for catching Rainbow Trout. Anglers often favor the early morning or late evening when the fish are most active. For a more guided experience, consider joining a local fishing charter, which offers expert knowledge and access to prime fishing locations that might be challenging to find on your own.

3. Techniques and Tips for Successful Fishing To make the most of your fishing trip, it's essential to understand the techniques that work best in Lake Tahoe. Trolling is a popular method, particularly for catching Mackinaw trout. If you're after Kokanee Salmon, consider using lures and downriggers to reach the cooler depths where they reside. Fly fishing is also a rewarding option, especially in the tributary streams around the lake.

4. Conservation and Catch-and-Release Practices Lake Tahoe's ecosystem is delicate, and anglers are encouraged to practice catch-and-release to help maintain the fish population and the overall health of the lake. Always check local regulations regarding fishing limits and seasons, and ensure you have the necessary fishing license before casting your line.

Wildlife Viewing: A Glimpse into Lake Tahoe's Biodiversity

1. Lake Tahoe's Diverse Wildlife Lake Tahoe is a haven for wildlife enthusiasts. The region boasts a rich array of animals, including black bears, mule deer, and a variety of bird species like bald eagles, ospreys, and mountain bluebirds. The surrounding forests and alpine meadows provide perfect habitats for these creatures, making wildlife viewing a rewarding activity year-round.

2. Top Wildlife Viewing Locations For those keen on observing wildlife, there are several hotspots around Lake Tahoe. Emerald Bay State Park offers excellent opportunities to see ospreys diving for fish, while Taylor Creek Visitor Center is a prime location for spotting bears and other wildlife, especially during the salmon spawning season. The Desolation Wilderness area is also a fantastic spot for encountering more elusive animals, like mountain lions and bobcats, though sightings are rare.

3. Best Times for Wildlife Viewing Wildlife activity varies throughout the year, but some of the best times to visit are during the early morning or late afternoon when animals are most active. In the spring and summer, migratory birds are abundant, and the local fauna is busy preparing for the upcoming seasons. Autumn is particularly special, as the fall foliage creates a breathtaking backdrop for wildlife watching, and the animals are often seen foraging in preparation for winter.

4. Tips for Responsible Wildlife Viewing Respecting the wildlife and their habitats is crucial for both your safety and the well-being of the animals. Keep a safe distance from all wildlife, use binoculars or a telephoto lens for close-up views, and never attempt to feed or approach animals. Stick to marked trails to minimize your impact on the environment, and be mindful of noise levels to avoid disturbing the natural behavior of the wildlife.

CHAPTER 6: FAMILY-FRIENDLY ACTIVITIES

6.1 Tahoe Treetop Adventure Park: Ziplining and Ropes Courses

Nestled in the scenic surroundings of Lake Tahoe, the Tahoe Treetop Adventure Park is a must-visit destination for families seeking a thrilling yet safe outdoor experience. This adventure park, renowned for its exhilarating zip lines and challenging ropes courses, offers a unique opportunity for families to bond, build confidence, and enjoy the beauty of nature from the treetops. Whether you're an adventure enthusiast or a first-timer looking for some fun, the park provides a range of activities that cater to all ages and skill levels.

Exploring the Ziplining Experience

1. Aerial Thrills for All Ages Ziplining at Tahoe Treetop Adventure Park is an exhilarating way to experience the forest from a bird's-eye view. The park features multiple zip lines of varying heights and lengths, ensuring that there's something for everyone, from young children to adults. Each zip line course is designed to provide a safe yet thrilling experience, allowing participants to soar through the treetops while taking in the breathtaking views of the Sierra Nevada mountains.

2. Safety First: What to Expect Safety is a top priority at Tahoe Treetop Adventure Park, making it a perfect activity for families. Before embarking on any zip line, participants are given a thorough safety briefing and fitted with harnesses, helmets, and other necessary gear. The park's staff are trained professionals who guide participants through every step, ensuring that everyone feels secure and confident before taking the leap. For younger children, there are gentler, lower-to-the-ground zip lines that offer the same thrill without the height.

3. A Variety of Courses to Choose From Tahoe Treetop Adventure Park boasts several zip line courses, each offering a different level of challenge and excitement. The "Bear Cub" course, for instance, is ideal for younger children, with lower platforms and shorter zip lines. For those seeking more adrenaline, the "Black Bear" and "Grizzly" courses offer longer, faster zip lines that span across the forest, providing an unforgettable rush as you glide through the air. Families can choose to complete multiple courses, making for a full day of adventure.

Conquering the Ropes Courses

1. Building Confidence and Teamwork The ropes courses at Tahoe Treetop Adventure Park are designed to challenge participants physically and mentally, making them an excellent activity for families looking to build teamwork and confidence. These courses feature a series of obstacles suspended between trees, including wobbly bridges, swinging logs, cargo nets, and more. Each course is a test of balance, agility, and problem-solving, providing a rewarding sense of accomplishment upon completion.

2. Tailored for All Skill Levels The ropes courses are categorized by difficulty, allowing participants to choose the right level based on their comfort and skill. The beginner courses, like the "Flying Squirrel" or "Chipmunk," are closer to the ground and feature easier obstacles, perfect for younger children or those new to ropes courses. For older kids and adults looking for more of a challenge, the intermediate and advanced courses, such as "Rattlesnake" or "Bobcat," offer higher platforms and more complex obstacles that require greater focus and determination.

3. Safety Measures and Guidance Just like with the zip lines, safety is paramount on the ropes courses. Participants are equipped with harnesses and securely attached to safety lines at all times. Instructors are stationed throughout the courses to offer assistance and encouragement, ensuring that everyone feels supported as they navigate the obstacles. The park's continuous belay system means that once you're clipped in, you're always connected, providing peace of mind for parents and participants alike.

A Day of Adventure: What Families Can Expect

1. Planning Your Visit Tahoe Treetop Adventure Park is a fantastic destination for a full day of family fun. It's recommended to plan your visit in advance, especially during peak seasons, as the park can get busy. Booking online is a convenient way to secure your spot and avoid long wait times. The park opens year-round, but it's essential to check weather conditions, as they can affect some activities.

2. What to Bring Comfortable clothing and sturdy shoes are a must for your day at the adventure park. Dress in layers, as temperatures can vary, and bring along water bottles and snacks to keep energized. The park provides all necessary safety gear, but families might want to bring their own gloves for added comfort on the ropes courses. Don't forget your camera – the treetop views make for excellent photo opportunities!

3. Creating Lasting Memories Tahoe Treetop Adventure Park offers more than just physical challenges; it's a place where families can create lasting memories. The shared experience of overcoming obstacles, cheering each other on, and soaring through the trees together fosters a strong sense of connection and accomplishment. Many families find that this adventure brings them closer, with plenty of stories and laughs to share long after the day is over.

6.2 KID-FRIENDLY BEACHES: SAFE AND FUN FOR ALL AGES

1. Kings Beach: A Family Favorite

Overview Kings Beach, located on the North Shore of Lake Tahoe, is one of the most popular family-friendly beaches in the area. The wide, sandy shoreline and gently sloping lake bed make it an ideal spot for young children to play safely. The beach is known for its warm, shallow waters, which are perfect for wading and splashing.

Kid-Friendly Features

- **Shallow Waters:** The gradual incline of the lakebed ensures that even the youngest children can enjoy the water safely.

- **Playground:** Kings Beach features a playground right on the sand, allowing kids to switch between water fun and climbing activities.

- **Picnic Areas:** Families can take advantage of the numerous picnic tables and BBQ grills, making it easy to enjoy a meal by the water.

- **Restroom Facilities:** Clean and accessible restrooms are available, which is a big plus for families with small children.

- **Lifeguards on Duty:** During the peak summer season, lifeguards are stationed at the beach, providing an extra layer of safety for parents.

Activities for Older Kids Kings Beach isn't just for the little ones. Older kids can enjoy paddleboarding, kayaking, and even jet skiing, with equipment rentals available on-site. The beach is also a great spot for building sandcastles, with its fine, soft sand.

---

2. Sand Harbor: Crystal Clear Waters and Stunning Scenery

Overview Sand Harbor, located on the Nevada side of Lake Tahoe, is famous for its picturesque views and exceptionally clear water. It's a favorite spot for families who want to enjoy a day at the beach in a safe and beautiful setting. The beach is part of Sand Harbor State Park, which means it's well-maintained and offers a range of amenities.

Kid-Friendly Features

- **Shallow Swimming Areas:** Sand Harbor's swimming areas are well-marked and shallow, making it a safe environment for young swimmers.

- **Gentle Waves:** The water is typically calm, with gentle waves that are perfect for kids to play in without being overwhelmed.

- **Designated Swimming Zones:** Buoys clearly mark the swimming zones, ensuring that kids stay within safe boundaries.

- **Interactive Visitor Center:** The on-site visitor center offers educational displays about the local environment and wildlife, which can be a fun and educational break from the sun.

- **Shade Areas:** There are plenty of shaded picnic spots under the pine trees, which provide a cool retreat from the sun.

Activities for Older Kids Older children and teens can enjoy snorkeling in the clear waters, where they might spot fish and other aquatic life. The large granite boulders near the shore are also perfect for climbing and exploring. Kayak and paddleboard rentals are available for those looking to explore further out into the lake.

---

3. Pope Beach: A Relaxing and Spacious Beach

Overview Pope Beach, situated on the South Shore of Lake Tahoe, offers a relaxing environment with a wide, sandy beach that's perfect for families. The beach is known for its peaceful atmosphere and stunning views of the surrounding mountains.

Kid-Friendly Features

- **Shallow Waters:** The gentle slope into the water makes Pope Beach an excellent spot for toddlers and younger kids to safely enjoy the lake.

- **Large Picnic Area:** The beach is equipped with a spacious picnic area complete with tables and BBQ grills, perfect for a family lunch.

- **Restrooms and Changing Facilities:** The beach provides clean restrooms and changing facilities, which are convenient for families with small children.

- **Bicycle Path:** A scenic bike path runs parallel to the beach, offering a safe and fun option for a family bike ride.

Activities for Older Kids Pope Beach is a great location for swimming and paddleboarding. The calm waters are ideal for beginners, and there are rental shops nearby where you can rent water sports equipment. The beach's expansive shoreline is perfect for beach games like volleyball or frisbee.

---

4. Zephyr Cove Beach: Fun-Filled Adventure

Overview Zephyr Cove Beach, located on the southeast shore of Lake Tahoe, offers a lively and active environment that's perfect for families with children of all ages. Known for its variety of water sports and activities, Zephyr Cove is a great spot for a fun-filled day at the beach.

Kid-Friendly Features

- **Safe Swimming Areas:** The beach offers designated swimming areas that are monitored, ensuring a safe environment for kids.

- **Boat Rentals:** Older kids and teens can rent paddleboats or go on a boat tour, while younger children can enjoy the shallow areas close to the shore.

- **Horseback Riding:** Adjacent to the beach, Zephyr Cove Stables offers horseback riding tours through the surrounding forest, providing a unique adventure for the whole family.

- **Beachside Dining:** The beach has a convenient beachside café where families can grab a bite to eat without leaving the sand.

- **Picnic Areas with BBQs:** There are designated picnic areas with BBQ grills, making it easy to cook up a family meal while enjoying the lake view.

Activities for Older Kids For families with adventurous older children, Zephyr Cove offers a range of activities such as parasailing, jet skiing, and even scenic cruises on a paddlewheel boat. The beach volleyball courts are also a hit, providing a fun way for kids to burn off energy.

---

5. Commons Beach: Community Vibes and Family Fun

Overview Located in Tahoe City, Commons Beach is a favorite among locals and visitors alike, offering a community-oriented environment that's perfect for families. The beach is known for its safe swimming areas and weekly summer concerts and movies, making it a vibrant spot for family entertainment.

Kid-Friendly Features

- **Playground on the Beach:** Commons Beach features a large playground right on the sand, complete with swings, slides, and climbing structures that keep kids entertained for hours.

- **Shallow Waters:** The beach has shallow, calm waters ideal for young children to safely wade and splash around.

- **Weekly Events:** During the summer months, the beach hosts free concerts and movie nights, turning the area into a lively hub of family-friendly entertainment.

- **Picnic and BBQ Areas:** Families can take advantage of the well-maintained picnic areas, many of which have BBQ grills and tables.

- **Lawn Areas:** The grassy areas surrounding the beach are perfect for picnics, games, and simply relaxing in the shade.

Activities for Older Kids Older children can enjoy kayaking or paddleboarding, with rentals available nearby. The bike path that runs through Tahoe City is also easily accessible from the beach, offering a great opportunity for a family bike ride along the lake's edge.

6.3 SNOW PLAY AND SLEDDING: WINTER FUN FOR THE WHOLE FAMILY

When winter blankets Lake Tahoe in snow, the region transforms into a magical wonderland perfect for family fun. Among the various winter activities, snow play and sledding stand out as some of the most enjoyable and accessible ways for families to experience the season's beauty. Whether you're a local or a visitor, Lake Tahoe offers numerous spots where you and your family can sled down snowy hills, build snowmen, and enjoy the crisp winter air.

Top Sledding and Snow Play Spots in Lake Tahoe

1. Granlibakken Tahoe: A Classic Family Favorite

Overview Granlibakken Tahoe, located just outside Tahoe City, is a premier destination for families seeking a safe and fun sledding experience. This historic resort offers a dedicated sledding hill that's ideal for children and parents alike. With its gentle slopes and convenient amenities, Granlibakken provides everything you need for a memorable day in the snow.

Kid-Friendly Features

- **Gentle Sledding Hill:** The sledding hill at Granlibakken is perfectly suited for young children, offering a gentle incline that provides just the right amount of speed without being too intimidating.

- **Sled Rentals:** If you don't have your own sleds, Granlibakken has you covered with on-site rentals, ensuring that everyone in the family can join in the fun.

- **Snow Play Area:** In addition to sledding, there's a snow play area where kids can build snow forts, have snowball fights, and simply enjoy the winter environment.

- **Warming Hut:** After a few runs down the hill, families can warm up in the cozy hut, where hot cocoa and snacks are available.

Why It's Great for Families Granlibakken's manageable size and friendly atmosphere make it a top choice for families with young children or those new to sledding. The convenience of having rentals and a warming hut on-site means you can focus on having fun without worrying about logistics.

---

2. Adventure Mountain Lake Tahoe: High-Energy Sledding Fun

Overview For families looking for a bit more adventure, Adventure Mountain Lake Tahoe offers some of the best sledding in the region. Located on Echo Summit, this popular snow park features a variety of sledding hills that cater to different skill levels, from beginners to thrill-seekers. With its expansive terrain and stunning views, Adventure Mountain is the perfect place to spend a winter day.

Kid-Friendly Features

- **Multiple Sledding Hills:** Adventure Mountain boasts over a dozen sledding hills of varying sizes, ensuring that there's something for every age and comfort level.

- **Sled Rentals and Sales:** Whether you need to rent a sled or want to purchase your own, the park offers a range of options to suit your needs.

- **Designated Snow Play Areas:** In addition to sledding, the park has designated areas where kids can engage in snowball fights, build snowmen, or simply play in the snow.

- **Restroom Facilities:** Clean and accessible restrooms are available on-site, which is always a plus for families.

Why It's Great for Families Adventure Mountain's wide variety of hills and large snow play areas make it an excellent choice for families with children of all ages. The park's layout allows older kids and adults to enjoy more challenging runs, while younger children can stick to the gentler slopes. Plus, the breathtaking views of Lake Tahoe and the surrounding mountains add an extra layer of enjoyment to your visit.

---

3. Tahoe Donner Snowplay: Safe and Structured Winter Fun

Overview Tahoe Donner Snowplay, located in Truckee, offers a structured environment for snow play and sledding that's perfect for families. This facility is operated by the Tahoe Donner Association and provides a safe, monitored space for children to enjoy winter activities. With groomed sledding hills, a snow play area, and a tubing hill, Tahoe Donner Snowplay is a one-stop destination for winter fun.

Kid-Friendly Features

- **Groomed Sledding Hills:** The sledding hills at Tahoe Donner are groomed daily to ensure a smooth ride, reducing the risk of bumps and tumbles.

- **Tubing Hill:** For families looking for a different kind of thrill, the tubing hill offers an exciting way to zip down the slopes.

- **Snowman Building Area:** There's a dedicated space for kids to build snowmen, igloos, and other snow creations, making it a great spot for creative play.

- **On-Site Staff:** The presence of on-site staff ensures that the sledding and snow play areas are safe and well-maintained throughout the day.

- **Snack Bar:** Warm up and recharge with hot beverages and snacks available at the on-site snack bar.

Why It's Great for Families Tahoe Donner Snowplay's focus on safety and structure makes it an ideal location for families, especially those with younger children. The groomed hills and staff supervision provide peace of mind, allowing parents to relax while their kids enjoy the snow. The variety of activities available ensures that there's something for everyone, from toddlers to teens.

---

4. North Tahoe Regional Park: A Local Gem

Overview Located in Tahoe Vista, the North Tahoe Regional Park is a hidden gem that offers free access to snow play and sledding. This community park is a favorite among locals and provides a laid-back environment where families can enjoy the winter weather without the crowds. The park features several sledding hills, open spaces for snow play, and stunning views of Lake Tahoe.

Kid-Friendly Features

- **Variety of Sledding Hills:** The park offers multiple sledding hills, ranging from gentle slopes for younger kids to steeper runs for more adventurous sledders.

- **Open Snow Play Areas:** There's plenty of open space for kids to engage in snowball fights, build snowmen, or just run around in the snow.

- **Scenic Views:** The park's elevated location provides spectacular views of Lake Tahoe, adding to the overall experience.

- **Picnic Areas:** Although it's winter, the park's picnic areas are still accessible, offering a spot to enjoy a family snack or lunch.

- **Pet-Friendly:** If your family includes a furry friend, North Tahoe Regional Park is pet-friendly, allowing dogs to join in on the winter fun.

Why It's Great for Families North Tahoe Regional Park is perfect for families looking for a more relaxed, budget-friendly option for snow play and sledding. The free access and variety of hills make it easy to spend a spontaneous day in the snow. Its local charm and beautiful setting make it a favorite for both residents and visitors.

---

5. Soda Springs Mountain Resort: A Winter Wonderland for Kids

Overview Soda Springs Mountain Resort, located just off I-80 near Donner Summit, is one of the most kid-friendly winter resorts in the Lake Tahoe area. Known for its extensive snow play areas and tubing lanes, Soda Springs is a fantastic destination for families with young children. The resort's "Planet Kids" zone is specifically designed for children under 8, offering a safe and fun environment for winter activities.

Kid-Friendly Features

- **Planet Kids Zone:** This dedicated area for children under 8 features mini-snowmobiles, tubing carousels, and gentle slopes, making it a winter wonderland for little ones.

- **Tube Town:** Older kids and adults can enjoy the thrill of tubing down the multiple lanes in Tube Town, complete with a lift that takes you back to the top.

- **Snow Play Area:** In addition to tubing, Planet Kids also offers areas for snow play, where kids can build snow forts, have snowball fights, and more.

- **Magic Carpet Lifts:** The resort features magic carpet lifts that make it easy for kids to get back up the hill after a run, ensuring they have more time for fun.

- **On-Site Amenities:** Soda Springs offers all the amenities a family needs for a day on the mountain, including restrooms, a café, and equipment rentals.

Why It's Great for Families Soda Springs Mountain Resort is designed with young families in mind. The focus on safe, age-appropriate activities ensures that even the youngest members of the family can enjoy the snow. The convenience of on-site amenities and the wide range of activities available make it a top choice for a day of winter fun.

Tips for a Safe and Enjoyable Sledding Experience

- **Dress Warmly:** Ensure everyone in the family is dressed in layers, with waterproof jackets, pants, gloves, and boots. Helmets are recommended, especially for young children.

- **Bring the Right Gear:** If you're bringing your own sleds, opt for sturdy models with brakes or steering capabilities. Avoid using makeshift sleds like garbage bags or plastic sheets, as they can be unsafe.

- **Safety First:** Always supervise children during sledding and snow play. Choose hills with a clear runout area at the bottom, free of obstacles like trees or rocks.

- **Time Your Visit:** To avoid crowds, consider visiting sledding areas early in the morning or on weekdays. This not only enhances your experience but also reduces wait times and the risk of collisions on the slopes.

- **Stay Hydrated:** Even in cold weather, it's important to stay hydrated. Bring along water and snacks to keep energy levels up throughout the day.

6.4 MUSEUMS AND EDUCATIONAL CENTERS: LEARNING THROUGH PLAY

The region boasts a variety of museums and educational centers designed to stimulate curiosity and foster a love of learning in children and adults alike. These venues offer interactive exhibits, hands-on activities, and engaging programs that make learning an exciting adventure. Whether your family is interested in history, science, or the natural environment, Lake Tahoe's museums and educational centers provide countless opportunities for learning through play.

---

1. Tahoe Science Center: Exploring Environmental Wonders

Overview The Tahoe Science Center, located in Incline Village, is a fantastic destination for families eager to learn about Lake Tahoe's unique ecosystem and the broader environmental science topics. Operated by the UC Davis Tahoe Environmental Research Center, this center offers a mix of interactive exhibits and educational programs that make complex scientific concepts accessible and engaging for all ages.

Kid-Friendly Features

- **3D Visualization Theater:** The center's 3D theater allows visitors to dive deep into Lake Tahoe's underwater world, exploring its geology, ecology, and the environmental challenges it faces. The immersive experience makes science both fun and educational for kids.

- **Hands-On Exhibits:** Children can engage with hands-on exhibits that demonstrate key environmental principles such as water clarity, invasive species, and climate change. These interactive displays encourage kids to learn by doing, making science tangible and understandable.

- **Interactive Touch Screens:** The center features touch screens that allow kids to explore various aspects of Lake Tahoe's environment, from its wildlife to its water quality. These screens provide a fun way for children to interact with information and explore topics at their own pace.

- **Special Programs and Workshops:** The Tahoe Science Center regularly hosts educational programs and workshops for children and families. These programs are designed to be both informative and enjoyable, offering opportunities for kids to engage with science in a playful way.

Why It's Great for Families The Tahoe Science Center is an excellent resource for families who want to combine education with play. The interactive exhibits and engaging programs ensure that children are not just passive learners but active participants in their educational journey. The focus on environmental stewardship also teaches kids the importance of caring for our planet, making this a valuable visit for the whole family.

---

2. KidZone Museum: A World of Imagination and Play

Overview The KidZone Museum, located in Truckee, is a beloved children's museum that offers a playful and educational environment for young kids. Designed for children aged 7 and under, the museum is filled with interactive exhibits that encourage imaginative play, creativity, and hands-on learning. It's a place where kids can explore, create, and learn in a setting that feels like one big playground.

Kid-Friendly Features

- **Indoor Play Structures:** The museum's indoor play areas are perfect for younger children. These structures are designed to stimulate physical activity while encouraging imaginative play. Kids can climb, slide, and explore to their heart's content.

- **Art Studio:** The museum's art studio is a space where kids can unleash their creativity. With various art supplies at their disposal, children can paint, draw, and craft, exploring their artistic side in a supportive environment.

- **Nature-Themed Exhibits:** The museum features nature-themed exhibits that allow children to learn about the natural world through play. These exhibits include a forest play area and a water table where kids can experiment with the flow of water, learning about its properties in a fun, hands-on way.

- **Reading Nook:** For quieter moments, the KidZone Museum offers a cozy reading nook filled with books for children of all ages. It's a great spot for parents and kids to relax together and enjoy a good story.

- **Outdoor Play Area:** During the warmer months, the museum's outdoor play area offers additional space for kids to run, climb, and explore. The area is designed to encourage physical activity and interaction with nature.

Why It's Great for Families The KidZone Museum is a perfect destination for families with young children looking for a safe, engaging space where learning and play go hand in hand. The variety of exhibits and activities ensures that there's something for every child to enjoy. Parents can join in the fun or sit back and watch as their kids explore and learn through play.

---

3. Gatekeeper's Museum: A Journey into Lake Tahoe's Past

Overview The Gatekeeper's Museum, located in Tahoe City, offers families a fascinating glimpse into the history of the Lake Tahoe region. Set in a replica of the original Gatekeeper's Cabin, this museum features exhibits that explore the cultural, historical, and natural heritage of the area. From

Native American artifacts to stories of early pioneers, the museum provides a rich educational experience for visitors of all ages.

Kid-Friendly Features

- **Washoe Indian Basket Collection:** One of the highlights of the museum is its collection of Washoe Indian baskets, considered one of the finest in the region. Kids can learn about the traditional crafts of the Washoe people and see firsthand the intricate designs and craftsmanship of these baskets.

- **Interactive History Exhibits:** The museum's exhibits are designed to be engaging and informative, with interactive elements that help bring history to life. Children can learn about the daily lives of early settlers, the construction of the transcontinental railroad, and the natural history of Lake Tahoe.

- **Children's Activity Area:** The museum offers a children's activity area where kids can participate in hands-on activities related to the exhibits. These activities might include crafts, puzzles, or games that make learning about history fun and interactive.

- **Outdoor Exploration:** The museum's location on the shores of Lake Tahoe provides ample opportunities for outdoor exploration. Families can take a stroll along the lake, visit the nearby Marion Steinbach Indian Basket Museum, or enjoy a picnic on the museum's grounds.

Why It's Great for Families The Gatekeeper's Museum offers a unique educational experience that connects children and families with the rich history of the Lake Tahoe region. The combination of indoor exhibits and outdoor exploration makes it an ideal destination for families looking to learn and play together. The museum's focus on local history and culture provides valuable context for understanding the Lake Tahoe area and its significance.

4. UC Davis Tahoe City Field Station: Science Meets Adventure

Overview The UC Davis Tahoe City Field Station, also known as the Historic Hatchery, is a research and educational facility that offers visitors a chance to learn about Lake Tahoe's ecology and environmental research. The station provides guided tours, educational programs, and interactive exhibits that make science accessible and fun for all ages.

Kid-Friendly Features

- **Historic Fish Hatchery:** The field station is housed in a historic fish hatchery building, where children can learn about the history of fish breeding in Lake Tahoe and the efforts to preserve the lake's native fish species.

- **Ecology Exhibits:** The field station features exhibits on Lake Tahoe's ecology, including its water quality, native species, and the impact of human activity on the environment. Interactive displays allow kids to engage with the material in a hands-on way.

- **Guided Nature Walks:** The field station offers guided nature walks that explore the surrounding area's natural environment. These walks are designed to be educational and engaging, with a focus on the local flora, fauna, and ecological processes.

- **Family Science Programs:** Throughout the year, the field station hosts family science programs that include workshops, hands-on activities, and interactive presentations. These programs are designed to inspire a love of science and nature in children and their families.

Why It's Great for Families The UC Davis Tahoe City Field Station is an excellent destination for families interested in science and the natural world. The combination of historical exhibits, interactive displays, and outdoor activities makes it a well-rounded educational experience. Families can learn about the important work being done to preserve Lake Tahoe's environment while enjoying the beautiful natural setting.

5. Watson Cabin Museum: A Glimpse into Pioneer Life

Overview The Watson Cabin Museum, located in Tahoe City, is one of the oldest log cabins still standing in the Lake Tahoe region. This small but charming museum offers a unique window into the life of early settlers in the area. Through its well-preserved interior and period artifacts, the Watson Cabin provides an intimate look at pioneer life in the early 20th century.

Kid-Friendly Features

- **Authentic Pioneer Home:** The Watson Cabin is a fully furnished pioneer home, complete with original furnishings and household items from the early 1900s. Kids can step back in time and see how families lived over a century ago.

- **Guided Tours:** The museum offers guided tours that are tailored to children's interests, with stories and explanations that make history come alive. Kids can learn about the daily routines of pioneer families, including cooking, cleaning, and making a living in the rugged Tahoe environment.

- **Hands-On Activities:** The museum occasionally offers hands-on activities for children, such as making traditional crafts or playing games from the pioneer era. These activities help kids connect with history in a tangible way.

- **Scenic Location:** The Watson Cabin's location near the shores of Lake Tahoe provides a picturesque backdrop for a family outing. After exploring the museum, families can enjoy a walk along the lake or visit nearby parks and trails.

Why It's Great for Families The Watson Cabin Museum is a hidden gem that offers a quiet, reflective experience for families interested in history. The intimate setting and well-preserved artifacts make it a fascinating place for children to explore the past. The museum's focus on everyday life in the early 20th century provides valuable insights into the challenges and triumphs of the region's early settlers.

CHAPTER 7: LOCAL CUISINE AND DINING

7.1 LAKEFRONT DINING: RESTAURANTS WITH A VIEW

One of the most memorable ways to experience the region is by dining at one of the many lakefront restaurants that offer breathtaking views of the crystal-clear waters and majestic mountains. Whether you're looking for a romantic dinner, a family-friendly meal, or a casual bite to eat, Lake Tahoe's lakefront dining options provide the perfect setting to enjoy delicious cuisine while soaking in the serene ambiance. Here's a detailed look at some of the best lakefront dining experiences in Lake Tahoe.

1. Edgewood Restaurant: Elegance on the Water

Overview Located on the south shore of Lake Tahoe, Edgewood Restaurant is part of the luxurious Edgewood Tahoe Resort. This fine dining establishment is celebrated for its upscale cuisine, impeccable service, and, of course, its stunning panoramic views of the lake. The restaurant's floor-to-ceiling windows allow diners to take in the breathtaking scenery, whether it's the vibrant colors of a sunset or the serene reflection of the moon on the water.

Cuisine Edgewood Restaurant offers a menu that blends classic American cuisine with contemporary flair, focusing on locally sourced ingredients. Signature dishes often include fresh seafood, prime steaks, and creative vegetarian options. The menu changes seasonally to reflect the freshest ingredients available.

Signature Dishes

- **Pan-Seared Scallops:** Perfectly cooked scallops served with a seasonal vegetable medley and a rich beurre blanc sauce.

- **Filet Mignon:** A tender cut of beef, grilled to perfection and served with garlic mashed potatoes and seasonal vegetables.

- **Wild Mushroom Risotto:** A creamy and flavorful risotto featuring locally foraged mushrooms, parmesan, and truffle oil.

Atmosphere Edgewood Restaurant exudes an air of sophistication, making it ideal for special occasions or a romantic evening out. The elegant decor, combined with the stunning views, creates a truly memorable dining experience. During the warmer months, the outdoor patio offers an even closer connection to the lake, with seating right at the water's edge.

Why It's a Must-Visit Edgewood Restaurant is a must-visit for anyone looking to combine fine dining with one of the best views in Lake Tahoe. The combination of exceptional food, attentive service, and an unparalleled lakefront location makes it a top choice for discerning diners.

2. The Boathouse on the Pier: Casual Dining with Unbeatable Sunsets

Overview The Boathouse on the Pier, located at the Beach Retreat & Lodge in South Lake Tahoe, offers a more casual dining experience without sacrificing the view. Situated directly on a pier that extends out into Lake Tahoe, this restaurant provides diners with a front-row seat to some of the most spectacular sunsets the region has to offer. The laid-back atmosphere, combined with the stunning views, makes it a favorite spot for both locals and visitors.

Cuisine The Boathouse on the Pier focuses on American comfort food with a twist, offering a menu that includes fresh seafood, burgers, salads, and more. The dishes are designed to be both satisfying and approachable, making it a great choice for families and groups.

Signature Dishes

- **Fish Tacos:** Freshly grilled fish served in warm tortillas with cabbage slaw, pico de gallo, and a tangy lime crema.

- **Boathouse Burger:** A juicy burger topped with bacon, cheddar cheese, lettuce, tomato, and a special house sauce, served with a side of crispy fries.

- **Clam Chowder:** A hearty bowl of creamy clam chowder, packed with tender clams and potatoes, perfect for enjoying on a cool Tahoe evening.

Atmosphere The Boathouse on the Pier offers a relaxed and welcoming atmosphere that's perfect for a casual meal. The indoor dining area is cozy and features large windows that frame the lake, while the outdoor seating on the pier provides an even closer connection to the water. The vibe is friendly and unpretentious, making it a great spot to unwind and enjoy the natural beauty of Lake Tahoe.

Why It's a Must-Visit The Boathouse on the Pier is a must-visit for anyone looking to enjoy a delicious meal in a casual setting with stunning lake views. The restaurant's location on the pier offers a unique perspective of Lake Tahoe, making it an ideal spot to watch the sunset while savoring comfort food.

3. Gar Woods Grill & Pier: Classic Tahoe Vibes

Overview Gar Woods Grill & Pier, located in Carnelian Bay on the north shore of Lake Tahoe, is a beloved institution known for its lively atmosphere, great food, and beautiful lakefront setting. Named after the famous boat designer Gar Wood, the restaurant exudes classic Tahoe charm, with a spacious deck that offers sweeping views of the lake. Whether you arrive by car or by boat, Gar Woods provides a quintessential Tahoe dining experience.

Cuisine Gar Woods specializes in California cuisine with an emphasis on fresh seafood and steaks. The menu features a mix of classic dishes and innovative creations, all prepared with high-quality ingredients. The restaurant is also famous for its Wet Woody cocktails, a must-try when dining here.

Signature Dishes

- **Coconut-Crusted Prawns:** Large prawns coated in a crispy coconut crust, served with a tangy orange-chili dipping sauce.

- **Gar Woods Filet:** A tender filet mignon grilled to perfection and served with garlic mashed potatoes and seasonal vegetables.

- **Crab Stuffed Artichoke:** A whole artichoke stuffed with a savory crab mixture, served with lemon aioli for dipping.

Atmosphere Gar Woods has a lively and inviting atmosphere that makes it a popular choice for both locals and tourists. The interior features rustic wood beams and large windows that offer stunning views of the lake. During the summer months, the expansive deck is the place to be, offering al fresco dining with unbeatable lake views. Live music often enhances the vibrant ambiance, making it a fun spot for both day and evening outings.

Why It's a Must-Visit Gar Woods Grill & Pier is a must-visit for anyone looking to experience the classic Tahoe vibe. The combination of great food, refreshing cocktails, and a lively atmosphere, all set against the backdrop of Lake Tahoe, makes it a memorable dining destination.

4. West Shore Café & Inn: Lakeside Elegance

Overview West Shore Café & Inn, located in Homewood on the west shore of Lake Tahoe, offers a refined yet relaxed dining experience with one of the most picturesque lakefront settings in the region. The café is part of a boutique inn, providing a cozy and intimate atmosphere perfect for a romantic dinner or a leisurely lunch. The restaurant's deck and pier offer some of the best views of Lake Tahoe, making it a popular spot for sunset dining.

Cuisine The menu at West Shore Café & Inn focuses on seasonal California cuisine with an emphasis on fresh, locally sourced ingredients. The dishes are elegantly presented and designed to showcase the flavors of the region. The restaurant also offers an extensive wine list featuring selections from California's top vineyards.

Signature Dishes

- **Seared Ahi Tuna:** Fresh ahi tuna seared to perfection and served with a wasabi aioli, pickled ginger, and a seaweed salad.

- **Wild Mushroom Risotto:** A creamy risotto made with a mix of wild mushrooms, truffle oil, and parmesan cheese.

- **Lobster Mac & Cheese:** A decadent take on a comfort food classic, featuring chunks of lobster in a rich, creamy cheese sauce.

Atmosphere West Shore Café & Inn exudes elegance with a warm, welcoming vibe. The interior features rustic wood accents, a stone fireplace, and large windows that frame the stunning lake views. The outdoor deck and pier seating offer a more casual option, where guests can dine under the stars with the sound of the water lapping against the shore. The service is attentive and friendly, adding to the overall charm of the experience.

Why It's a Must-Visit West Shore Café & Inn is a must-visit for those seeking an elegant yet relaxed dining experience on the shores of Lake Tahoe. The combination of exquisite food, impeccable service, and breathtaking views makes it a top choice for special occasions or simply enjoying the beauty of the lake.

---

5. Sunnyside Restaurant & Lodge: A Classic Tahoe Tradition

Overview Sunnyside Restaurant & Lodge, located on the west shore of Lake Tahoe, is a long-standing favorite known for its lively atmosphere, beautiful lakefront setting, and delicious food. With a history dating back to the 1940s, Sunnyside has become a Tahoe tradition, offering a welcoming spot for both locals and visitors to enjoy a meal by the water. The restaurant's large deck is one of the best places in Tahoe to take in the lake views while enjoying a casual meal.

Cuisine Sunnyside Restaurant & Lodge offers a menu that blends classic American cuisine with a touch of California flair. The dishes are made with fresh, seasonal ingredients and are designed to be both satisfying and approachable. The restaurant is also famous for its fish tacos and other seafood offerings.

Signature Dishes

- **Sunnyside Famous Fish Tacos:** Grilled or fried fish served in soft tortillas with cabbage slaw, pico de gallo, and a tangy lime crema.

- **Grilled Ribeye Steak:** A juicy ribeye steak cooked to order and served with garlic mashed potatoes and seasonal vegetables.

- **Ahi Poke:** Fresh ahi tuna marinated in a soy-ginger sauce, served with avocado, cucumber, and wonton crisps.

Atmosphere Sunnyside Restaurant & Lodge has a laid-back and inviting atmosphere that's perfect for families, groups, or anyone looking to enjoy a relaxed meal by the lake. The interior is warm and rustic, with wood-paneled walls and a large stone fireplace. The expansive deck is the star of the show, offering plenty of seating with stunning views of Lake Tahoe. In the summer, the deck is bustling with activity, making it a great spot to enjoy the lake's lively ambiance.

Why It's a Must-Visit Sunnyside Restaurant & Lodge is a must-visit for anyone looking to experience a classic Tahoe tradition. The combination of great food, a lively atmosphere, and a beautiful lakefront setting makes it a popular choice for both locals and visitors. Whether you're stopping by for lunch, dinner, or just a drink on the deck, Sunnyside offers a quintessential Tahoe experience.

7.2 FARM-TO-TABLE EXPERIENCES: FRESH, LOCAL FLAVORS

The farm-to-table movement has taken root in the region, with many restaurants and eateries emphasizing the importance of using locally grown produce, humanely raised meats, and freshly caught seafood. These establishments prioritize seasonal ingredients, often sourced from nearby farms, ranches, and waters, to create dishes that reflect the flavors of the Lake Tahoe area. Here's a guide to some of the best farm-to-table dining experiences in Lake Tahoe, where you can savor fresh, local flavors in every bite.

---

1. The Lake House: A Seasonal Feast of Local Goodness

Overview The Lake House, located in South Lake Tahoe, is a shining example of farm-to-table dining done right. This cozy, upscale restaurant takes pride in sourcing the freshest ingredients from local farms and purveyors. The menu changes frequently to reflect the seasons, ensuring that every dish is made with the highest quality produce, meats, and seafood available.

Cuisine The Lake House offers a contemporary American menu that highlights the best of the region's bounty. The chefs work closely with local farmers, ranchers, and fishermen to bring a taste of Lake Tahoe to the table. The dishes are thoughtfully prepared and beautifully presented, making every meal a culinary experience.

Signature Dishes

- **Seasonal Vegetable Risotto:** A creamy risotto made with fresh, seasonal vegetables, locally foraged mushrooms, and finished with a touch of truffle oil.

- **Grilled Sierra Nevada Trout:** Freshly caught trout from the Sierra Nevada, grilled to perfection and served with roasted fingerling potatoes and a lemon-caper butter sauce.

- **Farmers Market Salad:** A vibrant salad featuring a mix of organic greens, heirloom tomatoes, and cucumbers, tossed in a house-made vinaigrette and topped with local goat cheese.

Atmosphere The Lake House offers an intimate and elegant dining experience, with a warm and inviting ambiance that complements its farm-to-table ethos. The interior features rustic wood accents and soft lighting, creating a relaxed yet refined atmosphere. The restaurant's commitment to sustainability extends to its decor, with reclaimed wood and eco-friendly materials used throughout the space.

Why It's a Must-Visit The Lake House is a must-visit for those seeking a true farm-to-table experience in Lake Tahoe. The focus on locally sourced ingredients and seasonal dishes ensures that every meal is fresh, flavorful, and reflective of the region's agricultural richness.

---

2. Manzanita at The Ritz-Carlton: Luxury Meets Local Flavors

Overview Manzanita, located at The Ritz-Carlton in North Lake Tahoe, offers a luxurious farm-to-table dining experience that seamlessly blends gourmet cuisine with the freshest local ingredients. The restaurant's commitment to sustainability and quality is evident in every dish, with a menu that celebrates the flavors of the Sierra Nevada region.

Cuisine Manzanita's menu is a sophisticated take on California cuisine, with a strong emphasis on seasonality and local sourcing. The chefs work with nearby farms and ranches to curate a menu that highlights the best of what the region has to offer. From freshly picked vegetables to artisanal cheeses and sustainably raised meats, every ingredient is carefully selected to create dishes that are both innovative and delicious.

Signature Dishes

- **Herb-Crusted Rack of Lamb:** A tender rack of lamb encrusted with fresh herbs, served with a medley of roasted root vegetables and a red wine reduction.

- **Garden Herb Risotto:** A creamy risotto made with fresh herbs from the restaurant's own garden, served with seasonal vegetables and a parmesan crisp.

- **Pacific Halibut:** Sustainably sourced halibut, pan-seared and served with a citrus beurre blanc, accompanied by locally grown asparagus and fingerling potatoes.

Atmosphere Manzanita offers a dining experience that is both luxurious and inviting. The restaurant's interior features a modern design with natural elements that reflect the surrounding landscape. Floor-to-ceiling windows offer stunning views of the mountains, while the open kitchen allows diners to watch the chefs at work. The ambiance is sophisticated yet relaxed, making it an ideal spot for a special occasion or a romantic evening out.

Why It's a Must-Visit Manzanita is a must-visit for those looking to indulge in a high-end farm-to-table experience. The combination of luxurious surroundings, exceptional service, and a menu that celebrates local flavors makes it one of the premier dining destinations in Lake Tahoe.

---

3. Moody's Bistro Bar & Beats: Where Fresh Meets Fun

Overview Moody's Bistro Bar & Beats, located in the historic Truckee Hotel in Truckee, offers a unique farm-to-table experience that combines fresh, locally sourced ingredients with a lively atmosphere. Known for its innovative cuisine, craft cocktails, and live music, Moody's is a favorite among locals and visitors alike.

Cuisine Moody's focuses on New American cuisine with a farm-to-table twist. The chefs are passionate about using organic, sustainably sourced ingredients to create dishes that are both flavorful and inventive. The menu changes frequently to incorporate the freshest seasonal ingredients available, ensuring that each visit offers something new and exciting.

Signature Dishes

- **Grass-Fed Burger:** A juicy burger made with grass-fed beef from a local ranch, topped with caramelized onions, sharp cheddar, and house-made pickles, served with hand-cut fries.

- **Seasonal Flatbread:** A rotating selection of flatbreads featuring seasonal ingredients such as heirloom tomatoes, local mushrooms, and artisanal cheeses.

- **House-Made Charcuterie Board:** An assortment of house-made charcuterie, including cured meats, pâtés, and local cheeses, served with pickles, mustard, and freshly baked bread.

Atmosphere Moody's offers a fun and vibrant dining experience with a rustic-chic ambiance that's both welcoming and stylish. The restaurant features a cozy interior with exposed brick walls, wooden beams, and an open kitchen. The lively bar area is perfect for enjoying a craft cocktail or local beer, while the dining room offers a more intimate setting. On weekends, live jazz and blues performances add to the energetic vibe, making Moody's a great place to enjoy a night out.

Why It's a Must-Visit Moody's Bistro Bar & Beats is a must-visit for those looking to experience fresh, local flavors in a fun and lively setting. The combination of inventive cuisine, a relaxed atmosphere, and live music makes it a standout in Lake Tahoe's dining scene.

---

4. PlumpJack Café: Farm-to-Table Elegance in Squaw Valley

Overview PlumpJack Café, located in Squaw Valley, offers a refined farm-to-table dining experience that emphasizes the use of local, organic ingredients. The café is part of the PlumpJack Squaw Valley Inn, a boutique hotel known for its commitment to sustainability and quality. The restaurant's menu is designed to showcase the best of Northern California's bounty, with a focus on fresh, seasonal ingredients.

Cuisine PlumpJack Café's menu is a celebration of California cuisine, with dishes that highlight the flavors of the region's farms, ranches, and vineyards. The chefs work closely with local purveyors to source the freshest ingredients, from organic vegetables to sustainably raised meats. The result is a menu that is both sophisticated and approachable, with dishes that are beautifully presented and full of flavor.

Signature Dishes

- **Grilled Sonoma Duck Breast:** A succulent duck breast grilled to perfection and served with wild rice pilaf, roasted seasonal vegetables, and a cherry-port reduction.

- **Butternut Squash Ravioli:** House-made ravioli filled with creamy butternut squash, served with brown butter, sage, and shaved parmesan.

- **Pan-Roasted Chicken:** A tender chicken breast pan-roasted with garlic and herbs, served with roasted root vegetables and a light pan jus.

Atmosphere PlumpJack Café offers an elegant yet relaxed dining experience, with a warm and inviting ambiance that makes it perfect for a special evening out. The interior features contemporary decor with rustic touches, such as wooden beams and stone accents, that reflect the natural beauty of the surrounding mountains. Large windows offer views of Squaw Valley, adding to the restaurant's serene atmosphere.

Why It's a Must-Visit PlumpJack Café is a must-visit for those seeking an elegant farm-to-table dining experience in Lake Tahoe. The restaurant's commitment to sustainability, combined with its exceptional cuisine and inviting atmosphere, makes it a top choice for discerning diners.

---

5. Cottonwood Restaurant & Bar: A Taste of Tahoe's History

Overview Cottonwood Restaurant & Bar, located in a historic ski lodge overlooking Truckee, offers a farm-to-table dining experience that is rich in both flavor and history. The restaurant is known for its use of fresh, local ingredients and its commitment to sustainability. With its cozy ambiance and stunning views, Cottonwood is a favorite spot for both locals and visitors.

Cuisine Cottonwood's menu is a blend of contemporary American cuisine and traditional comfort food, with a strong emphasis on fresh, seasonal ingredients. The chefs work with local farmers, ranchers, and fishermen to create dishes that are both satisfying and reflective of the region's culinary heritage.

Signature Dishes

- **Braised Short Ribs:** Tender short ribs braised in a rich red wine sauce, served with creamy mashed potatoes and roasted seasonal vegetables.

- **Rainbow Trout Almondine:** Fresh rainbow trout from local waters, pan-seared and topped with toasted almonds and lemon-butter sauce, served with wild rice and sautéed greens.

- **Buttermilk Fried Chicken:** Crispy buttermilk fried chicken served with house-made biscuits, honey butter, and a side of coleslaw.

Atmosphere Cottonwood Restaurant & Bar offers a warm and welcoming atmosphere that reflects its historic roots. The interior features rustic wood beams, a stone fireplace, and vintage ski memorabilia that give the space a cozy, mountain lodge feel. The restaurant's hilltop location provides panoramic views of Truckee and the surrounding mountains, making it a perfect spot for a sunset dinner.

Why It's a Must-Visit Cottonwood Restaurant & Bar is a must-visit for those looking to experience Lake Tahoe's farm-to-table movement in a setting steeped in history. The combination of fresh, local ingredients, a cozy atmosphere, and stunning views makes it a dining experience you won't want to miss.

7.3 BEST BREAKFAST AND BRUNCH SPOTS: START YOUR DAY RIGHT

Whether you're gearing up for a day on the slopes, preparing for a hike, or simply looking to indulge in a leisurely morning meal, Lake Tahoe has an array of breakfast and brunch spots that offer delicious food, cozy atmospheres, and stunning views. From hearty mountain breakfasts to creative brunch dishes, here's a guide to some of the best places in Lake Tahoe to start your day right.

1. Fire Sign Café: A Local Favorite for Breakfast Classics

Overview Fire Sign Café, located in Tahoe City on the west shore of Lake Tahoe, is a beloved local institution that has been serving up hearty breakfasts and brunches since 1978. Known for its friendly service, cozy atmosphere, and generous portions, Fire Sign Café is the perfect spot to enjoy a classic American breakfast with a Tahoe twist.

Menu Highlights Fire Sign Café offers a menu full of breakfast staples made from scratch using fresh, locally sourced ingredients. From fluffy pancakes to savory omelets, there's something to satisfy every craving.

Signature Dishes

- **Fire Sign Eggs Benedict:** Two poached eggs served on a toasted English muffin with Canadian bacon, topped with rich hollandaise sauce, and served with home fries.

- **Blueberry Pancakes:** Fluffy pancakes filled with fresh blueberries, served with warm maple syrup and a side of whipped butter.

- **Huevos Rancheros:** A hearty plate of two eggs served over corn tortillas with black beans, salsa, avocado, and sour cream, topped with melted cheese.

Atmosphere Fire Sign Café exudes a warm, welcoming vibe that makes you feel right at home. The interior is charmingly rustic, with wooden tables, cozy booths, and local artwork adorning the walls. The café also offers outdoor seating on the patio, where you can enjoy your meal with a view of the surrounding pines.

Why It's a Must-Visit Fire Sign Café is a must-visit for anyone looking to enjoy a classic breakfast or brunch in a cozy, laid-back setting. The combination of delicious food, generous portions, and friendly service makes it a favorite among both locals and visitors.

---

2. The Red Hut Café: A Tahoe Tradition

Overview The Red Hut Café is a Tahoe staple with several locations around the lake, including South Lake Tahoe and Stateline. Established in 1959, The Red Hut Café is known for its retro diner vibe, classic American breakfasts, and welcoming atmosphere. It's the kind of place where you can expect a hearty meal and a dose of nostalgia.

Menu Highlights The Red Hut Café serves up all the breakfast classics you'd expect from a diner, with an emphasis on hearty portions and made-from-scratch goodness. The menu includes everything from waffles and pancakes to omelets and breakfast sandwiches.

Signature Dishes

- **Red Hut Waffle:** A golden, crispy waffle served with whipped butter, warm maple syrup, and your choice of fresh fruit or bacon.

- **Eggs & Bacon:** A classic breakfast plate featuring two eggs cooked to your liking, crispy bacon, hash browns, and toast.

- **Red Hut Special:** A breakfast sandwich made with two eggs, bacon or sausage, and cheese, served on a toasted English muffin or biscuit.

Atmosphere The Red Hut Café offers a charming, retro diner atmosphere with red vinyl booths, vintage signage, and a friendly, old-school vibe. The walls are decorated with memorabilia that reflects the café's long history in Lake Tahoe, adding to its nostalgic appeal.

Why It's a Must-Visit The Red Hut Café is a must-visit for those who appreciate classic American diner food served in a fun, retro setting. The combination of great food, friendly service, and a bit of Tahoe history makes it a memorable spot for breakfast or brunch.

3. The Log Cabin Caffe: Cozy and Charming in Kings Beach

Overview The Log Cabin Caffe, located in Kings Beach, is a quaint and charming breakfast spot housed in a cozy log cabin. Known for its homestyle cooking and welcoming atmosphere, The Log Cabin Caffe is a great place to enjoy a leisurely breakfast or brunch while soaking in the rustic charm of Lake Tahoe.

Menu Highlights The Log Cabin Caffe offers a menu filled with comforting breakfast favorites, all made with fresh, high-quality ingredients. The portions are generous, and the dishes are prepared with a homestyle touch that makes you feel like you're enjoying a meal at Grandma's house.

Signature Dishes

- **Stuffed French Toast:** Thick slices of French toast stuffed with cream cheese and fresh berries, topped with powdered sugar and served with warm maple syrup.

- **Log Cabin Skillet:** A hearty skillet breakfast featuring eggs, potatoes, bacon, sausage, onions, and bell peppers, topped with melted cheese and served with toast.

- **Banana Nut Pancakes:** Fluffy pancakes filled with ripe bananas and chopped walnuts, served with butter and syrup.

Atmosphere The Log Cabin Caffe is as cozy as it sounds, with a warm and inviting interior that features log walls, wooden tables, and a stone fireplace. The rustic decor and intimate setting make it a perfect spot for a relaxing morning meal. The café also offers outdoor seating on the patio, where you can enjoy your breakfast in the fresh mountain air.

Why It's a Must-Visit The Log Cabin Caffe is a must-visit for anyone looking to enjoy a cozy, homestyle breakfast in a charming, rustic setting. The combination of hearty, delicious food and a welcoming atmosphere makes it a favorite among locals and visitors alike.

4. Base Camp Café: A Brunch Lover's Paradise in Tahoe City

Overview Base Camp Café, located in Tahoe City, is a popular spot for breakfast and brunch, known for its creative dishes and vibrant atmosphere. The café is committed to using fresh, locally sourced ingredients to create a menu that's both innovative and satisfying. Whether you're fueling up for a day of adventure or enjoying a leisurely brunch with friends, Base Camp Café has something for everyone.

Menu Highlights Base Camp Café offers a diverse menu that includes both classic and contemporary breakfast dishes. The chefs are known for their creative takes on traditional brunch favorites, often incorporating unique ingredients and flavors.

Signature Dishes

- **Avocado Toast:** Fresh avocado spread on toasted artisan bread, topped with poached eggs, cherry tomatoes, radishes, and a drizzle of balsamic glaze.

- **Campfire Benedict:** A twist on the classic Eggs Benedict, featuring smoked salmon, poached eggs, and hollandaise sauce served on a toasted English muffin, with a side of home fries.

- **Breakfast Burrito:** A hearty burrito filled with scrambled eggs, bacon, potatoes, cheddar cheese, and salsa, served with sour cream and guacamole.

Atmosphere Base Camp Café offers a lively and welcoming atmosphere, with a modern yet rustic interior that reflects the adventurous spirit of Lake Tahoe. The café's large windows provide plenty of natural light, creating a bright and cheerful dining space. The outdoor patio is a popular spot during the warmer months, offering a relaxed setting to enjoy your meal with a view of the surrounding mountains.

Why It's a Must-Visit Base Camp Café is a must-visit for brunch lovers looking for fresh, creative dishes in a vibrant, welcoming setting. The café's commitment to quality ingredients and innovative flavors makes it a standout spot for breakfast or brunch in Lake Tahoe.

---

5. Café Biltmore: Classic Brunch with a Modern Twist

Overview Café Biltmore, located in the historic Biltmore Lodge & Casino in Crystal Bay, offers a delightful brunch experience that combines classic dishes with modern flair. The café is known for its extensive brunch menu, which features everything from hearty breakfast plates to lighter, more contemporary options. With its elegant setting and delicious food, Café Biltmore is a great place to start your day.

Menu Highlights Café Biltmore's menu offers a wide range of brunch options, from traditional breakfast favorites to more inventive dishes that cater to a variety of tastes. The café's chefs use fresh, locally sourced ingredients to create dishes that are both flavorful and satisfying.

Signature Dishes

- **Crab Cake Benedict:** A luxurious take on Eggs Benedict, featuring house-made crab cakes topped with poached eggs and hollandaise sauce, served with a side of home fries.

- **Belgian Waffles:** Light and crispy Belgian waffles served with fresh berries, whipped cream, and warm maple syrup.

- **Smoked Salmon Platter:** A plate of smoked salmon served with capers, red onions, cream cheese, and a toasted bagel, perfect for a lighter brunch option.

Atmosphere Café Biltmore offers a chic and modern dining experience with a touch of classic elegance. The café's interior features contemporary decor with comfortable seating, creating a relaxed yet stylish atmosphere. Large windows provide plenty of natural light, and the outdoor patio offers additional seating with views of the surrounding area.

Why It's a Must-Visit Café Biltmore is a must-visit for those looking to enjoy a classic brunch with a modern twist. The combination of elegant surroundings, a diverse menu, and exceptional service makes it a top choice for a leisurely weekend brunch in Lake Tahoe.

7.4 APRÈS-SKI AND APRÈS-ADVENTURE: PUBS, BREWERIES, AND CAFÉS

After a day of adventure, there's no better way to unwind than by enjoying the vibrant après-ski and après-adventure scene that the region has to offer. Whether you're in the mood for a craft beer, a cozy cup of coffee, or a lively pub atmosphere, Lake Tahoe has a variety of spots where you can relax and recharge. Here's a guide to some of the best pubs, breweries, and cafés for your après-ski and après-adventure needs.

---

1. The Bridgetender Tavern and Grill: A Classic Après-Ski Pub

Overview Located in Tahoe City, The Bridgetender Tavern and Grill is a beloved local pub known for its welcoming atmosphere, hearty food, and great drinks. Situated along the Truckee River, this classic après-ski spot offers a cozy indoor setting and a spacious outdoor patio, making it a perfect place to relax after a day on the slopes or trails.

Menu Highlights The Bridgetender is famous for its burgers, but the menu also features a wide variety of pub favorites, including sandwiches, salads, and appetizers. The bar offers a solid selection of craft beers, wines, and signature cocktails.

Signature Dishes and Drinks

- **BT Burger:** A juicy, half-pound burger topped with your choice of cheese, lettuce, tomato, onion, and pickles, served with a side of crispy fries.

- **Buffalo Wings:** Classic wings tossed in your choice of sauce, served with celery sticks and blue cheese dressing.

- **Truckee River Lemonade:** A refreshing cocktail made with vodka, lemonade, and a splash of soda, perfect for sipping on the patio.

Atmosphere The Bridgetender has a laid-back and friendly vibe that makes it a favorite among locals and visitors alike. The interior is warm and rustic, with wooden beams, a stone fireplace, and plenty of seating. The outdoor patio, which overlooks the Truckee River, is a great spot to enjoy a drink while soaking in the scenery.

Why It's a Must-Visit The Bridgetender Tavern and Grill is a must-visit for those looking to unwind in a classic pub setting after a day of adventure.

The combination of great food, a welcoming atmosphere, and a scenic location makes it an ideal spot for après-ski or après-hike relaxation.

---

2. Alibi Ale Works: A Brewery with Tahoe Flavor

Overview Alibi Ale Works is a popular craft brewery with locations in Incline Village and Truckee, offering a range of creative and delicious beers brewed right in Lake Tahoe. Known for its laid-back vibe and community-oriented atmosphere, Alibi Ale Works is the perfect spot to enjoy a post-adventure pint with friends.

Beer Selection Alibi Ale Works produces a diverse lineup of beers, including IPAs, stouts, lagers, and more. The brewery prides itself on using high-quality ingredients and experimenting with unique flavors, resulting in beers that are both innovative and approachable.

Signature Beers

- **Tahoe Pale Ale:** A balanced and refreshing pale ale with notes of citrus and pine, perfect for après-ski.

- **Porter in Paradise:** A smooth and rich porter with hints of chocolate and coffee, ideal for warming up after a day on the mountain.

- **Alibi IPA:** A hop-forward IPA with bold flavors of tropical fruit and a crisp finish.

Atmosphere Alibi Ale Works offers a relaxed and inviting atmosphere that's perfect for winding down after an active day. The brewery's taprooms feature communal tables, comfortable seating, and live music on weekends. The Truckee location also has a spacious outdoor beer garden, complete with fire pits and lawn games.

Why It's a Must-Visit Alibi Ale Works is a must-visit for craft beer enthusiasts looking to enjoy local brews in a welcoming and fun environment. The brewery's commitment to quality and creativity, combined with its lively atmosphere, makes it a top choice for après-ski and après-adventure gatherings.

---

3. Himmel Haus: Bavarian-Style Après-Ski Fun

Overview Himmel Haus, located near the base of Heavenly Mountain Resort in South Lake Tahoe, offers a unique après-ski experience with its Bavarian-inspired atmosphere, hearty German food, and extensive beer selection. This lively spot is known for its festive ambiance and is a great place to gather with friends after a day on the slopes.

Menu Highlights Himmel Haus serves up a menu full of traditional Bavarian dishes, including sausages, schnitzels, and pretzels. The beer list is equally impressive, featuring a wide selection of German and European brews, as well as local craft beers.

Signature Dishes and Drinks

- **Jägerschnitzel:** A breaded pork cutlet served with mushroom gravy, red cabbage, and spaetzle, a perfect post-ski comfort meal.

- **Bratwurst Plate:** A classic bratwurst sausage served with sauerkraut, mustard, and potato salad.

- **German Beers:** Himmel Haus offers a rotating selection of German beers on tap, including favorites like Paulaner Hefeweizen, Bitburger Pilsner, and Weihenstephaner Festbier.

Atmosphere Himmel Haus offers a cozy and festive atmosphere that transports you straight to Bavaria. The interior features rustic wooden tables, a large bar, and plenty of Bavarian decor. The lively vibe is enhanced by regular events such as live music, trivia nights, and beer tastings, making it a fun spot to hang out with friends.

Why It's a Must-Visit Himmel Haus is a must-visit for those looking to experience a Bavarian-style après-ski experience in Lake Tahoe. The combination of hearty German food, a fantastic beer selection, and a lively atmosphere makes it a unique and enjoyable spot to unwind after a day of adventure.

---

4. Blue Angel Café: Cozy Café with Global Flavors

Overview Blue Angel Café, located in South Lake Tahoe, offers a cozy and eclectic setting for après-ski or après-adventure relaxation. Known for its globally inspired menu and warm, inviting atmosphere, Blue Angel Café is a great place to enjoy a casual meal or a comforting cup of coffee after a day outdoors.

Menu Highlights Blue Angel Café's menu features a diverse selection of dishes inspired by cuisines from around the world. The café is known for its creative and flavorful offerings, including everything from hearty soups and sandwiches to fresh salads and international specialties.

Signature Dishes and Drinks

- **Lamb Gyro:** Tender lamb served in a warm pita with tzatziki, lettuce, tomato, and onion, accompanied by a side of sweet potato fries.

- **Curry Chicken Bowl:** A flavorful bowl of chicken simmered in a rich curry sauce, served over jasmine rice with a side of naan bread.

- **Hot Chocolate:** A rich and creamy hot chocolate, perfect for warming up after a day in the snow.

Atmosphere Blue Angel Café offers a cozy and laid-back atmosphere that's perfect for relaxing after a day of adventure. The café's interior is warm and inviting, with comfortable seating, soft lighting, and local artwork on the walls. The outdoor patio, complete with heaters and blankets, provides a charming setting for enjoying a meal or drink under the stars.

Why It's a Must-Visit Blue Angel Café is a must-visit for those looking to enjoy a cozy and eclectic après-ski experience in Lake Tahoe. The café's diverse menu, combined with its welcoming atmosphere, makes it a great spot for a casual meal or a relaxing drink after a day on the mountain.

---

5. CoffeeBar: A Café for the Coffee Connoisseur

Overview CoffeeBar, with locations in Truckee and Reno, is the perfect spot for those who appreciate a great cup of coffee and a relaxed, community-oriented atmosphere. Whether you're warming up after a day on the slopes or recharging after a hike, CoffeeBar offers a welcoming space to enjoy high-quality coffee, tea, and light bites.

Coffee and Menu Highlights CoffeeBar prides itself on serving expertly crafted coffee made from ethically sourced beans. The café also offers a selection of teas, pastries, and light meals, all made with fresh, high-quality ingredients.

Signature Drinks and Bites

- **Cappuccino:** A classic cappuccino made with expertly steamed milk and rich, flavorful espresso, perfect for a post-adventure pick-me-up.

- **Matcha Latte:** A creamy and energizing matcha latte made with high-quality matcha powder and steamed milk.

- **Avocado Toast:** A simple yet delicious avocado toast topped with sea salt, red pepper flakes, and a drizzle of olive oil, served on freshly baked bread.

Atmosphere CoffeeBar offers a modern and comfortable atmosphere, with plenty of seating, natural light, and a community-focused vibe. The café's interior is stylish yet unpretentious, making it a great spot to relax, catch up with friends, or get some work done. The outdoor seating areas, available in both locations, provide a lovely setting to enjoy your coffee with a view of the surrounding landscape.

Why It's a Must-Visit CoffeeBar is a must-visit for coffee lovers and anyone looking to enjoy a relaxed and welcoming après-ski or après-adventure experience. The café's commitment to quality and community, combined with its cozy atmosphere, makes it a top choice for a morning brew or an afternoon break in Lake Tahoe.

CHAPTER 8: CULTURAL EXPERIENCES AND LOCAL TRADITIONS

8.1 ART GALLERIES AND STUDIOS: TAHOE'S CREATIVE SCENE

Tahoe's art scene is a tapestry woven with diverse influences—ranging from the pristine landscapes that inspire breathtaking landscapes to the unique cultural heritage of the region. The galleries and studios around the lake are not just places to view art; they are creative hubs where artists, locals, and visitors alike come together to celebrate and explore artistic expression.

MUST-VISIT ART GALLERIES IN LAKE TAHOE

1. **Marcus Ashley Fine Art Gallery (South Lake Tahoe)** Located in the heart of South Lake Tahoe; the Marcus Ashley Fine Art Gallery is a cornerstone of the local art community. The gallery features an eclectic mix of works from both established and emerging artists. Whether you're drawn to contemporary paintings, sculptures, or glasswork, this gallery offers something for every art lover. It's a place where Tahoe's natural beauty is often interpreted in vibrant

and innovative ways, making it a must-see for anyone interested in how the environment influences local art.

2. **North Tahoe Arts (Tahoe City)** North Tahoe Arts is a nonprofit organization dedicated to supporting the local arts community. Their gallery in Tahoe City is a welcoming space where visitors can view and purchase works by local artists. Exhibitions rotate regularly, ensuring there's always something new to see. The gallery also hosts events, workshops, and classes, making it a vibrant hub for artistic expression and community engagement.

3. **Riverside Studios (Truckee)** Situated in the historic town of Truckee, Riverside Studios is a collective of local artists who have come together to share their work in a unique, collaborative environment. The studio and gallery showcase a diverse range of art forms, including ceramics, jewelry, photography, and painting. The laid-back atmosphere and the chance to meet the artists in their creative space make Riverside Studios a unique destination for art enthusiasts.

4. **Tahoe Art Haus & Cinema (Tahoe City)** While primarily known as a cinema, Tahoe Art Haus & Cinema also doubles as a gallery space where local artists display their work. The combination of film and art creates a culturally rich environment that offers a unique experience for visitors. It's an ideal spot for those who appreciate visual arts in all its forms, from independent films to local artwork.

EXPLORING THE STUDIOS: MEET THE ARTISTS

In addition to galleries, Lake Tahoe is home to several working studios where visitors can watch artists at work and even participate in creating their art. These studios offer a more intimate glimpse into the creative process, allowing visitors to connect directly with the artists.

1. **Atelier (Truckee)** Atelier is more than just a studio; it's a community space where art, culture, and creativity converge. The

studio offers workshops and classes in various mediums, from painting and printmaking to fiber arts and jewelry. Visiting Atelier provides an opportunity to learn new skills, meet local artists, and take home a piece of Tahoe's creative spirit.

2. **Alpenglow Art Studios (Kings Beach)** Tucked away in the charming town of Kings Beach, Alpenglow Art Studios offers visitors the chance to explore a working studio space. The studio focuses on ceramics and pottery, with classes available for all skill levels. Watching the artists transform raw materials into beautiful pieces of art is a mesmerizing experience that highlights the skill and dedication of Tahoe's artistic community.

3. **Truckee Roundhouse Makerspace (Truckee)** The Truckee Roundhouse is a nonprofit makerspace that fosters creativity across various disciplines, from woodworking and metalworking to textiles and digital arts. It's a place where artists and makers of all levels can collaborate, experiment, and bring their ideas to life. The Roundhouse often hosts open studios, giving visitors a behind-the-scenes look at the creative process in action.

ENGAGING WITH TAHOE'S CREATIVE SCENE

Visiting Lake Tahoe's art galleries and studios is more than just a visual experience—it's an opportunity to engage with the local culture on a deeper level. Many of these spaces host workshops, artist talks, and community events, providing a platform for meaningful exchanges between artists and visitors. Whether you're an art connoisseur or simply curious, Tahoe's creative scene invites you to explore, learn, and be inspired by the artistic expressions that make this region so unique.

8.2 MUSIC AND FILM FESTIVALS: YEAR-ROUND EVENTS

These events celebrate the region's artistic spirit, drawing both locals and visitors to experience the best in live performances, cinematic showcases, and more. Here's a look at some of the standout festivals that make Lake Tahoe a year-round cultural hotspot.

WINTER FESTIVALS: THE MAGIC OF MUSIC IN THE SNOW

1. **SnowGlobe Music Festival (South Lake Tahoe)** Held every December, the SnowGlobe Music Festival is one of the most anticipated winter events in Lake Tahoe. This three-day outdoor festival merges music with the region's winter wonderland, offering an eclectic lineup of electronic dance music, hip-hop, and indie performances. Attendees can enjoy live sets while surrounded by snow-covered landscapes, creating a unique and exhilarating experience. SnowGlobe also features art installations, fireworks, and a variety of food and drink vendors, making it a full sensory experience that keeps festival-goers coming back year after year.

2. **WinterWonderGrass (Palisades Tahoe)** Celebrating bluegrass music in the heart of winter, WinterWonderGrass is a festival that combines the love of music with a passion for the outdoors. Held in March, this event features top bluegrass, folk, and roots music artists performing against the stunning backdrop of the Sierra Nevada mountains. The festival also emphasizes sustainability, with a focus on local food, craft beer, and environmental consciousness. It's a family-friendly event where the music is as pure and refreshing as the mountain air.

SPRING AND SUMMER: MUSIC UNDER THE SUN

1. **Lake Tahoe Reggae Festival (South Lake Tahoe)** As the snow melts and the summer sun emerges, Lake Tahoe Reggae Festival brings the island vibes to the mountains. This one-day festival in July features a lineup of reggae's biggest names, attracting fans of all ages. Set at the Hard Rock Hotel & Casino's outdoor arena, the

festival offers a laid-back atmosphere where attendees can dance, relax, and soak up the sun. The event also includes local food vendors, craft booths, and a lively, welcoming community spirit.

2. **Valhalla Art, Music & Theatre Festival (South Lake Tahoe)** Running from June through September, the Valhalla Art, Music & Theatre Festival is one of Tahoe's most beloved summer traditions. Hosted at the historic Valhalla Estate, this festival offers a diverse lineup of music performances, theatrical productions, and art exhibits. The beautiful lakefront setting provides the perfect backdrop for enjoying everything from classical music concerts to jazz and blues performances. The festival's broad appeal makes it a favorite for both locals and visitors looking for cultural enrichment in a picturesque setting.

3. **Lake Tahoe Shakespeare Festival (Sand Harbor)** Although not a music festival in the traditional sense, the Lake Tahoe Shakespeare Festival deserves a mention for its cultural significance and the unique blend of theatre and live music it offers. Held at Sand Harbor State Park in July and August, the festival features world-class performances of Shakespearean plays, accompanied by live music that sets the mood for each scene. The open-air venue, with the backdrop of Lake Tahoe's clear waters and the Sierra Nevada, provides an unforgettable experience for theatre and music lovers alike.

AUTUMN: CELEBRATING FILM IN TAHOE

1. **Tahoe Film Fest (North Lake Tahoe)** As the summer crowds fade and the fall colors take over, the Tahoe Film Fest emerges as a celebration of independent cinema. Held in early December, this festival showcases a curated selection of environmental films, American independent movies, and Latin American cinema. The festival's mission is to raise awareness about the environment, which aligns perfectly with Lake Tahoe's reputation as a natural wonder. Screenings are held at various venues around North Lake

Tahoe, providing a cozy, intimate setting for film enthusiasts to gather and discuss the art of cinema.

2. **Mountainfilm on Tour (Truckee)** Mountainfilm on Tour brings the best of the Telluride Mountainfilm Festival to Lake Tahoe every November. This touring festival features documentaries focused on environmental, cultural, and social issues, as well as outdoor adventure films that inspire and educate. The event is a must-see for those who love the great outdoors and are passionate about preserving the natural world. The screenings in Truckee offer a chance to experience these powerful films in a community-oriented setting, followed by discussions that often include filmmakers and featured adventurers.

YEAR-ROUND MUSICAL EXPERIENCES

1. **Classical Tahoe (Incline Village)** For those who appreciate classical music, Classical Tahoe offers a series of year-round events that culminate in a summer festival each July and August. This festival brings together world-renowned musicians for a series of intimate performances that celebrate the rich traditions of classical music. Held at the Sierra Nevada College campus in Incline Village, the festival's concerts are known for their exceptional quality and the unique opportunity to see top-tier musicians in a stunning, serene environment.

2. **Live at Lakeview Summer Music Series (South Lake Tahoe)** The Live at Lakeview Summer Music Series is a free weekly event held every Thursday evening from June through August at Lakeview Commons. This community-focused series features a diverse lineup of live music, from rock and reggae to bluegrass and funk. The concerts take place right on the beach, offering spectacular views of Lake Tahoe as the sun sets. It's a perfect way to unwind after a day of exploring, with food trucks, local craft vendors, and a beer garden adding to the festive atmosphere.

8.3 Native American Heritage: Understanding the Washoe Tribe

For thousands of years, the Washoe people lived in harmony with the land, developing a profound spiritual connection to the lake they called "Da ow ga," which means "the lake" in their native language. Understanding the Washoe Tribe's heritage offers a glimpse into the region's past and provides valuable insights into the cultural significance of Lake Tahoe.

The Washoe Tribe: A Brief History

The Washoe Tribe, or Wašíšiw as they are known in their language, are indigenous to the Great Basin region, primarily residing in what is now known as western Nevada and eastern California. The tribe is composed of three main groups: the northern, southern, and eastern bands, each with its distinct territories and seasonal migration patterns.

Lake Tahoe was central to the Washoe people's way of life. They considered the lake a sacred place and believed it was the home of their ancestors. The Washoe would spend summers in the Lake Tahoe Basin, fishing, hunting, and gathering resources. Winters were spent in lower elevations, where the climate was milder.

Cultural Practices and Traditions

The Washoe Tribe's culture is rooted in a deep respect for the natural world. Their traditional way of life was based on hunting, fishing, and gathering, with an emphasis on sustainable practices that ensured the land and its resources were preserved for future generations.

1. **Basketry**: One of the most celebrated aspects of Washoe culture is their basketry. Washoe baskets are renowned for their intricate designs and craftsmanship. These baskets were not only functional but also held spiritual significance. Women of the tribe were the primary basket weavers, and the skill was passed down through

generations. Today, Washoe basketry is recognized as an important cultural art form, and the baskets are highly valued both within and outside the tribe.

2. **Language**: The Washoe language, Wašíšiw ʔítʔiw, is a unique language isolate, meaning it is not related to any other known language. Language is a crucial aspect of Washoe identity, and efforts have been made to revitalize and preserve it. The tribe has implemented programs to teach the language to younger generations, ensuring that this key part of their cultural heritage is not lost.

3. **Spiritual Beliefs**: The Washoe people have a spiritual connection to the land, particularly to Lake Tahoe. They believe that the lake is a sacred site and that it plays a central role in their creation stories. Traditional Washoe religion is animistic, with a belief in the spiritual presence in all natural things, including animals, plants, and geographical features.

4. **Social Structure**: The Washoe Tribe was traditionally organized into family groups, with social structure based on kinship and reciprocity. Leadership was not hierarchical but rather based on consensus, with decisions made collectively by the group. This communal approach extended to their resource management practices, where cooperation ensured the sustainability of their environment.

CHALLENGES AND RESILIENCE

The arrival of European settlers in the mid-19th century brought significant challenges to the Washoe people. The discovery of gold and silver in the region led to an influx of settlers, which resulted in the displacement of the Washoe from their ancestral lands. The exploitation of natural resources, particularly logging and fishing, further disrupted their traditional way of life.

Despite these challenges, the Washoe Tribe has shown remarkable resilience. They have worked tirelessly to preserve their cultural heritage and maintain their connection to Lake Tahoe. Today, the Washoe Tribe of Nevada and California is a federally recognized tribe with a government that advocates for the rights and interests of its people.

THE WASHOE TODAY: PRESERVING HERITAGE AND PROMOTING AWARENESS

The Washoe Tribe remains active in efforts to preserve their culture and educate others about their history. They continue to play a vital role in the Lake Tahoe community, particularly in environmental conservation efforts. The tribe collaborates with local organizations to protect the lake and its surrounding areas, ensuring that the natural beauty and cultural significance of the region are maintained for future generations.

1. **Cultural Preservation**: The Washoe Tribe has established cultural centers and programs to preserve and promote their heritage. These initiatives include language revitalization, traditional arts and crafts, and the sharing of oral histories. The tribe also hosts events and ceremonies that allow members to connect with their culture and share it with the wider community.

2. **Environmental Stewardship**: The Washoe people's traditional knowledge of the land is invaluable in contemporary conservation efforts. The tribe works closely with environmental groups to manage and protect the Lake Tahoe Basin. This partnership reflects the Washoe's enduring commitment to caring for the land that has sustained them for millennia.

3. **Educational Outreach**: The Washoe Tribe is involved in educational outreach programs that aim to raise awareness about their history, culture, and the importance of Lake Tahoe to their people. These programs often include presentations, workshops, and guided tours that highlight the Washoe's historical connection to the region.

Visiting Washoe Cultural Sites

For those interested in learning more about the Washoe Tribe and their connection to Lake Tahoe, there are several cultural sites and events to explore:

1. **Tahoe Maritime Museum (Homewood, CA)**: The Tahoe Maritime Museum features exhibits on the Washoe Tribe, including artifacts, photographs, and educational displays that provide insight into their historical relationship with the lake.

2. **Valhalla Tahoe (South Lake Tahoe, CA)**: The Washoe Cultural Foundation often hosts events and exhibitions at Valhalla Tahoe, offering visitors a chance to experience Washoe culture through storytelling, music, and traditional crafts.

3. **Annual Wa She Shu It' Deh Festival (Carson City, NV)**: This annual event celebrates Washoe culture with traditional dances, music, crafts, and food. The festival is an opportunity for the public to engage with the Washoe community and learn about their traditions.

8.4 Local Markets and Craft Fairs: Unique Souvenirs and Gifts

Whether you're searching for handcrafted items that reflect the area's natural beauty or locally made products that tell a story, these markets offer a rich variety of options. From one-of-a-kind artworks to artisanal foods, exploring these markets is not only a shopping experience but also an opportunity to connect with the local culture and support Tahoe's talented artisans.

Tahoe City Farmers Market (Tahoe City, CA)

The Tahoe City Farmers Market is more than just a place to pick up fresh produce—it's a vibrant community gathering spot where locals and visitors alike come to browse, shop, and socialize. Held every Thursday from May to October at Commons Beach, this market offers stunning views of Lake Tahoe while you peruse the stalls.

What to Expect:

- **Local Artisans**: In addition to fresh fruits and vegetables, the market features a variety of handmade goods, including jewelry, pottery, and woodcrafts. These items make perfect souvenirs, reflecting the natural materials and craftsmanship of the region.

- **Gourmet Treats**: Pick up some locally produced honey, jams, or baked goods to take a taste of Tahoe home with you. Many of these products are made with ingredients sourced from the surrounding area, ensuring authenticity and quality.

- **Live Music**: The market often hosts live music performances, adding to the festive atmosphere. It's a great place to enjoy some tunes while exploring the various stalls.

TRUCKEE THURSDAYS (TRUCKEE, CA)

Truckee Thursdays is a beloved summer tradition that transforms the historic downtown Truckee into a bustling street fair. Running from mid-June to mid-August, this weekly event is a celebration of local culture, creativity, and community.

What to Expect:

- **Crafts and Art**: Truckee Thursdays is known for its wide selection of local art and craft vendors. You'll find everything from hand-painted ceramics and metalwork to unique clothing and accessories. Many artisans are on hand to discuss their work, providing insight into the creative process.

- **Food and Drink**: The event features a food court with a variety of local food trucks and vendors offering everything from gourmet grilled cheese sandwiches to craft beers. It's a great place to try regional specialties and grab a bite to eat while you shop.

- **Family-Friendly Fun**: With activities for kids, including face painting and games, Truckee Thursdays is a family-friendly event that offers something for everyone.

HEAVENLY VILLAGE CRAFT FAIR (SOUTH LAKE TAHOE, CA)

The Heavenly Village Craft Fair, held throughout the summer and during the holiday season, is a go-to destination for finding high-quality, handcrafted items. Located in the heart of South Lake Tahoe, this fair is an excellent place to discover unique gifts and souvenirs.

What to Expect:

- **Handmade Jewelry**: Many local artisans specialize in creating stunning jewelry that incorporates natural elements like turquoise, silver, and semi-precious stones. These pieces make for meaningful keepsakes or thoughtful gifts.

- **Art and Photography**: The craft fair features a range of visual arts, including paintings, photography, and prints that capture the beauty of Lake Tahoe's landscapes. These artworks are perfect for bringing a piece of Tahoe's natural splendor into your home.

- **Holiday Shopping**: During the winter season, the craft fair takes on a festive atmosphere, with holiday-themed items, ornaments, and gifts. It's an ideal spot to find unique Christmas presents that you won't see anywhere else.

VALHALLA HOLIDAY FAIRE (SOUTH LAKE TAHOE, CA)

For those visiting Lake Tahoe during the winter months, the Valhalla Holiday Faire is a must-see event. Held at the historic Valhalla Tahoe Grand

Hall, this annual craft fair is a celebration of the holiday season and local craftsmanship.

What to Expect:

- **Artisan Goods**: The Holiday Faire features a curated selection of local artisans offering everything from handcrafted candles and soaps to textiles and woodworking. These items are perfect for unique, thoughtful holiday gifts.

- **Festive Atmosphere**: The event is set in the beautifully decorated Grand Hall, with roaring fires, holiday music, and seasonal treats adding to the charm. It's a wonderful way to get into the holiday spirit while supporting local makers.

- **Kids' Activities**: The Valhalla Holiday Faire often includes activities for children, such as ornament-making workshops and visits with Santa Claus, making it a festive outing for the whole family.

MADE IN TAHOE FESTIVAL (SQUAW VALLEY, CA)

The Made in Tahoe Festival, held annually over Memorial Day weekend, is a celebration of all things local. Hosted at Palisades Tahoe (formerly Squaw Valley), this festival showcases the talents of the Tahoe community with a wide variety of products made by local artisans.

What to Expect:

- **Locally Made Products**: From handcrafted furniture and home décor to gourmet foods and natural beauty products, the Made in Tahoe Festival is the ultimate shopping destination for those looking to support local businesses. Each vendor is carefully selected to ensure quality and authenticity.

- **Live Entertainment**: The festival features live performances from local musicians, dancers, and entertainers, providing a lively backdrop as you shop and explore.

- **Interactive Booths**: Many artisans offer demonstrations or workshops at their booths, allowing visitors to see the creative process firsthand. This interactive element adds depth to your shopping experience and allows you to connect with the makers on a personal level.

SOUTH LAKE TAHOE FLEA MARKET (SOUTH LAKE TAHOE, CA)

The South Lake Tahoe Flea Market is a weekend event that takes place from May through September, offering a mix of antiques, collectibles, and crafts. Located on U.S. Highway 50, this market is a great spot to find eclectic and vintage items that make for one-of-a-kind souvenirs.

What to Expect:

- **Vintage Finds**: The flea market is known for its selection of vintage items, from retro home décor to classic Tahoe memorabilia. If you're a fan of antiques, this is the place to hunt for treasures.

- **Handmade Crafts**: Alongside the antiques, you'll find stalls featuring handmade crafts, including knitted goods, woodworking, and jewelry. These items offer a unique, personal touch that mass-produced souvenirs lack.

- **Bargain Hunting**: Part of the fun at the flea market is the thrill of finding a great deal. With a wide range of prices, you're sure to find something that fits your budget.

CHAPTER 9: ACCOMMODATION GUIDE

9.1 Luxury Resorts and Mountain Lodges

From opulent resorts with every amenity imaginable to cozy mountain lodges that blend comfort with rustic charm, Lake Tahoe's top-tier accommodations provide the perfect base for exploring the area. Here's a guide to some of the best luxury resorts and mountain lodges in Lake Tahoe, including their key features, costs, addresses, and the pros and cons of each.

1. The Ritz-Carlton, Lake Tahoe

Cost: Starting at $900 per night
Address: 13031 Ritz-Carlton Highlands Court, Truckee, CA 96161
Website: Ritz-Carlton, Lake Tahoe

Pros:

- **Ski-in/Ski-out Access:** Direct access to Northstar California Resort's ski slopes makes this an ideal choice for winter sports enthusiasts.

- **Luxury Amenities:** The Ritz-Carlton offers world-class amenities, including a full-service spa, multiple fine dining options, a heated outdoor pool, and a state-of-the-art fitness center.

- **Exceptional Service:** Known for its impeccable service, the Ritz-Carlton ensures every guest feels pampered from the moment they arrive.

- **Family-Friendly:** The hotel offers a variety of activities for children, including a dedicated kids' club and family-friendly outdoor adventures.

Cons:

- **High Cost:** The luxury experience comes with a hefty price tag, making it one of the more expensive options in Lake Tahoe.

- **Remote Location:** While perfect for those seeking a secluded retreat, the Ritz-Carlton is somewhat removed from the action of South Lake Tahoe, which may require additional travel for those looking to explore the area's nightlife and shopping.

2. EDGEWOOD TAHOE RESORT

Cost: Starting at $700 per night
Address: 100 Lake Parkway, Stateline, NV 89449
Website: Edgewood Tahoe Resort

Pros:

- **Lakefront Location:** Situated right on the shores of Lake Tahoe, Edgewood offers stunning lake views from many of its rooms and suites.

- **World-Class Golf:** The resort is home to a championship golf course, offering a top-notch experience for golf enthusiasts.

- **Upscale Dining:** Edgewood boasts several fine dining options, including the renowned Edgewood Restaurant, known for its exceptional cuisine and panoramic lake views.

- **Spa and Wellness:** The on-site spa offers a range of treatments that incorporate natural ingredients and reflect the tranquility of the Tahoe environment.

Cons:

- **Seasonal Crowds:** Due to its prime location and popularity, the resort can be crowded during peak seasons, particularly in summer and winter.

- **Pricey Dining:** While the dining options are exceptional, they are also quite expensive, which can add to the overall cost of the stay.

3. The Landing Resort & Spa

Cost: Starting at $600 per night
Address: 4104 Lakeshore Blvd, South Lake Tahoe, CA 96150
Website: The Landing Resort & Spa

Pros:

- **Boutique Luxury:** The Landing offers a more intimate experience with just 82 rooms, each elegantly appointed with high-end furnishings and modern amenities.

- **Lakefront Access:** Located right on the lake, guests enjoy easy access to the beach and breathtaking views of the water and surrounding mountains.

- **Gourmet Dining:** The on-site restaurant, Jimmy's, offers a fine dining experience with a menu that emphasizes locally sourced ingredients.

- **Personalized Service:** As a smaller resort, The Landing is known for its personalized service, ensuring that guests' needs are met with attention to detail.

Cons:

- **Limited On-Site Activities:** Unlike larger resorts, The Landing does not offer a wide range of on-site activities, which may be a drawback for those looking for a more comprehensive resort experience.

- **Parking Fees:** The resort charges additional fees for parking, which can add to the overall cost of the stay.

4. The Resort at Squaw Creek

Cost: Starting at $500 per night
Address: 400 Squaw Creek Road, Olympic Valley, CA 96146
Website: Resort at Squaw Creek

Pros:

- **Ski-in/Ski-out Access:** This resort is perfect for winter sports enthusiasts, with direct access to the slopes of Palisades Tahoe (formerly Squaw Valley).

- **Family-Friendly:** The resort offers a range of family-friendly activities, including an outdoor heated pool, ice skating, and a kids' camp.

- **Dining Options:** Multiple dining options on-site, including a fine dining restaurant and casual eateries, provide variety and convenience for guests.

- **Scenic Location:** Nestled in Olympic Valley, the resort offers spectacular views of the surrounding mountains and easy access to outdoor activities year-round.

Cons:

- **Outdated Decor:** While the resort offers many amenities, some areas and rooms may feel slightly dated compared to newer luxury accommodations.

- **Can Be Crowded:** The resort's popularity can lead to crowds, especially during peak ski season, which may impact the overall experience.

5. HYATT REGENCY LAKE TAHOE RESORT, SPA AND CASINO

Cost: Starting at $450 per night
Address: 111 Country Club Drive, Incline Village, NV 89451
Website: Hyatt Regency Lake Tahoe

Pros:

- **All-Inclusive Amenities:** The Hyatt Regency offers a full range of amenities, including a casino, spa, multiple dining options, and a private beach.

- **Family-Friendly:** With a dedicated kids' club, a family pool, and a range of outdoor activities, the resort caters well to families.

- **Lake Access:** The resort's private beach on Lake Tahoe provides a secluded and serene environment for relaxation.

- **Moderate Pricing:** Compared to other luxury resorts in the area, the Hyatt Regency offers a more affordable option without compromising on amenities and service.

Cons:

- **Casino Atmosphere:** While the casino can be a draw for some, it may not appeal to all guests, particularly those looking for a quieter, more nature-focused retreat.

- **Older Property:** Some parts of the resort may show signs of wear and age, though the property is well-maintained overall.

6. PLUMPJACK INN

Cost: Starting at $400 per night
Address: 1920 Squaw Valley Road, Olympic Valley, CA 96146
Website: PlumpJack Inn

Pros:

- **Cozy Boutique Experience:** PlumpJack Inn offers a warm and welcoming environment with the feel of a luxury boutique hotel. Its smaller size allows for personalized service and a more intimate atmosphere.

- **Excellent Dining:** The inn's on-site restaurant, PlumpJack Cafe, is well-regarded for its farm-to-table cuisine and extensive wine list.

- **Proximity to Skiing:** Located in Olympic Valley, the inn provides easy access to skiing and other outdoor activities.

- **Dog-Friendly:** PlumpJack Inn is one of the few luxury accommodations in the area that is dog-friendly, making it a great choice for travelers with pets.

Cons:

- **Limited Amenities:** While the inn offers a cozy, intimate experience, it does not have the extensive amenities of larger resorts, such as a spa or fitness center.

- **Seasonal Variability:** The atmosphere and offerings at the inn may vary significantly depending on the season, with winter attracting more ski-oriented guests.

7. THE LODGE AT EDGEWOOD TAHOE

Cost: Starting at $850 per night
Address: 180 Lake Parkway, Stateline, NV 89449
Website: The Lodge at Edgewood Tahoe

Pros:

- **Luxurious Accommodations:** The Lodge at Edgewood Tahoe offers spacious, elegantly designed rooms and suites with high-end amenities, including fireplaces and private balconies with lake views.

- **Exclusive Setting:** The lodge's location on the Edgewood Golf Course provides a serene and picturesque setting, perfect for relaxation.

- **On-Site Dining:** Multiple dining options, including the upscale Bistro Edgewood, offer a range of culinary experiences without leaving the property.

- **Eco-Friendly Initiatives:** The lodge is committed to sustainability, with eco-friendly practices incorporated throughout the property, including energy-efficient lighting, water conservation, and recycling programs.

Cons:

- **High Price Point:** As one of the most luxurious options in Lake Tahoe, the Lodge at Edgewood comes with a correspondingly high price tag, which may be out of reach for some travelers.

- **Limited Nightlife:** While the lodge offers a peaceful retreat, those looking for vibrant nightlife may need to venture into nearby South Lake Tahoe.

9.2 BOUTIQUE HOTELS AND COZY CABINS

1. BASECAMP TAHOE SOUTH

Cost: Starting at $200 per night
Address: 4143 Cedar Ave, South Lake Tahoe, CA 96150
Website: Basecamp Tahoe South

Pros:

- **Adventure-Inspired Design:** Basecamp Tahoe South is designed with the outdoor enthusiast in mind, offering a blend of modern comforts and rustic charm. The rooms feature cozy decor with a nod to camping and adventure.

- **Central Location:** Located just a short walk from the Heavenly Gondola and the lake, this boutique hotel is perfectly situated for exploring South Lake Tahoe's attractions.

- **Social Spaces:** The hotel offers inviting communal areas, including a rooftop hot tub with lake views, a beer garden, and fire pits for evening s'mores.

- **Eco-Friendly:** Basecamp is committed to sustainability, with eco-friendly practices such as energy-efficient lighting and water conservation measures.

Cons:

- **Limited Amenities:** While the hotel is charming and well-located, it lacks some of the amenities of larger resorts, such as a full-service spa or on-site dining.

- **Noisy at Times:** Due to its central location and popularity with younger travelers, it can be a bit noisy during peak seasons.

2. THE COTTAGE INN

Cost: Starting at $250 per night
Address: 1690 W Lake Blvd, Tahoe City, CA 96145
Website: The Cottage Inn

Pros:

- **Charming Atmosphere:** The Cottage Inn is a delightful collection of individually themed cottages, each with its own unique decor and character. The rustic yet elegant ambiance makes it a perfect romantic getaway.

- **Beach Access:** Located just steps from the lake, guests have direct access to a private beach, perfect for swimming or relaxing by the water.

- **Complimentary Breakfast:** A homemade, complimentary breakfast is served daily, offering a cozy start to the day with options like fresh-baked pastries and gourmet coffee.

- **Adults-Only:** This adults-only inn ensures a peaceful and serene environment, ideal for couples or those seeking a quiet retreat.

Cons:

- **No On-Site Dining:** While the inn offers a lovely breakfast, there are no on-site dining options for lunch or dinner. However, there are several restaurants nearby.

- **Limited Availability:** Due to its small size and popularity, The Cottage Inn often books up quickly, especially during peak seasons.

3. CEDAR GLEN LODGE

Cost: Starting at $275 per night
Address: 6589 N Lake Blvd, Tahoe Vista, CA 96148
Website: Cedar Glen Lodge

Pros:

- **Award-Winning Charm:** Cedar Glen Lodge has received numerous accolades for its charming accommodations and friendly service. The property features a mix of cabins and lodge rooms, each beautifully appointed with rustic yet luxurious touches.

- **On-Site Amenities:** The lodge offers a range of amenities, including a heated outdoor pool, hot tub, sauna, and fire pits. There's also a wine bar and a cozy lounge area.

- **Sustainability Focus:** The property is eco-friendly, with sustainable practices such as solar power, electric car charging stations, and water conservation measures.

- **Close to Attractions:** Located in Tahoe Vista, Cedar Glen Lodge is close to both North Tahoe's beaches and ski resorts, making it a convenient base for year-round activities.

Cons:

- **Pricey During Peak Seasons:** Rates can be on the higher side during peak seasons, such as summer and winter holidays.

- **Small Property:** While the small size adds to its charm, it may lack some of the expansive amenities found at larger resorts.

4. Fireside Lodge Bed and Breakfast

Cost: Starting at $250 per night
Address: 515 Emerald Bay Rd, South Lake Tahoe, CA 96150
Website: Fireside Lodge

Pros:

- **Cozy, Rustic Atmosphere:** Fireside Lodge offers a warm, cabin-like experience with rooms featuring log furniture, stone fireplaces, and woodland-themed decor.

- **Pet-Friendly:** The lodge is pet-friendly, making it a great choice for travelers who want to bring their furry friends along.

- **Complimentary Amenities:** Guests enjoy a complimentary breakfast, afternoon snacks, and access to bikes, snowshoes, and sleds depending on the season.

- **Family-Owned:** The lodge is family-owned and operated, which contributes to its welcoming and personalized service.

Cons:

- **Location on a Busy Road:** The lodge is located on Emerald Bay Road, which can be busy and noisy at times. However, the rooms are well-insulated, minimizing this issue.

- **Limited Space:** As a smaller property, there are fewer communal spaces and amenities compared to larger hotels.

5. Tahoma Meadows Cottages

Cost: Starting at $225 per night
Address: 6821 West Lake Blvd, Tahoma, CA 96142
Website: Tahoma Meadows

Pros:

- **Charming Cottages:** Tahoma Meadows offers a variety of individual cottages, each with its own unique decor and cozy atmosphere. The rustic charm and private setting make it ideal for a romantic getaway or a peaceful retreat.

- **Proximity to Nature:** Located on the West Shore of Lake Tahoe, the cottages are close to hiking trails, state parks, and the lake itself, offering easy access to outdoor activities.

- **Pet-Friendly:** The property is pet-friendly, and some cottages come with fenced yards, perfect for those traveling with dogs.

- **Complimentary Breakfast:** A complimentary homemade breakfast is served daily, featuring delicious options like quiche, fresh fruit, and pastries.

Cons:

- **Limited Modern Amenities:** While the cottages are charming and comfortable, they are more rustic, with fewer modern amenities like air conditioning or high-end electronics.

- **No On-Site Dining:** Aside from breakfast, there are no on-site dining options, so guests will need to venture out for meals.

6. THE COACHMAN HOTEL

Cost: Starting at $180 per night
Address: 4100 Pine Blvd, South Lake Tahoe, CA 96150
Website: The Coachman Hotel

Pros:

- **Modern Aesthetic:** The Coachman Hotel offers a blend of modern design with a retro twist. Rooms are sleek and stylish, with contemporary furnishings and decor that appeal to younger travelers and design enthusiasts.

- **Central Location:** Located in South Lake Tahoe, The Coachman is just a short walk from the Heavenly Gondola, the lake, and the Stateline casinos, making it a convenient option for exploring the area.

- **Social Atmosphere:** The hotel features communal spaces like an outdoor pool, hot tub, and a bar serving craft beers and coffee. Evening s'mores by the fire pit are a guest favorite.

- **Affordability:** Compared to other boutique options, The Coachman offers more budget-friendly rates, making it an attractive choice for those seeking style without breaking the bank.

Cons:

- **Limited Privacy:** The social nature of the hotel, with communal spaces and close quarters, may not appeal to those seeking a more private or quiet experience.

- **Minimalist Amenities:** While stylish, the rooms are more minimalist in terms of amenities, with fewer luxuries compared to other boutique hotels.

7. BLACK BEAR LODGE

Cost: Starting at $300 per night
Address: 1202 Ski Run Blvd, South Lake Tahoe, CA 96150
Website: Black Bear Lodge

Pros:

- **Luxurious Log Cabin Experience:** Black Bear Lodge offers a luxurious take on the log cabin experience, with beautifully appointed rooms and private cabins that feature high-end finishes, stone fireplaces, and plush bedding.

- **Intimate Setting:** With only a handful of rooms and cabins, the lodge offers a private and serene environment, perfect for couples or those seeking a peaceful retreat.

- **Convenient Location:** The lodge is located near Heavenly Ski Resort and just a short drive from the lake, offering easy access to both winter and summer activities.

- **Personalized Service:** The small size of the lodge allows for personalized attention, with a focus on guest comfort and satisfaction.

Cons:

- **High Cost:** The luxury experience at Black Bear Lodge comes with a higher price tag, making it one of the more expensive boutique options in the area.

- **Limited Availability:** Due to its small size and popularity, the lodge often books up quickly, especially during peak seasons.

8. TAHOE MOUNTAIN LODGING

Cost: Starting at $350 per night
Address: 4001 Northstar Dr, Truckee, CA 96161
Website: Tahoe Mountain Lodging

Pros:

- **Spacious Accommodations:** Tahoe Mountain Lodging offers a range of luxury condos and vacation homes, each equipped with full kitchens, living areas, and private balconies. This is an excellent option for families or groups seeking more space and privacy.

- **Ski-In/Ski-Out Access:** Located at Northstar California Resort, these lodgings offer direct access to the slopes, making them ideal for ski vacations.

- **High-End Amenities:** Properties feature upscale amenities such as heated pools, hot tubs, fitness centers, and concierge services.

- **Year-Round Appeal:** In addition to skiing, the location offers easy access to hiking, mountain biking, and other outdoor activities in the summer.

Cons:

- **Expensive:** These luxury accommodations come at a premium price, especially during ski season or peak summer months.

- **Resort Fees:** Additional resort fees may apply, which can increase the overall cost of the stay.

9.3 BUDGET-FRIENDLY ACCOMMODATIONS

1. LAKE TAHOE VACATION RESORT BY DIAMOND RESORTS

Cost: Starting at $100 per night
Address: 901 Ski Run Blvd, South Lake Tahoe, CA 96150
Website: Lake Tahoe Vacation Resort

Pros:

- **Great Location:** The resort is conveniently located near the lake, Heavenly Ski Resort, and the casinos at Stateline, offering easy access to many of Lake Tahoe's attractions.

- **Spacious Rooms:** The resort offers a variety of room types, including studios and suites with kitchenettes, making it ideal for longer stays or families.

- **Amenities:** Despite its budget-friendly rates, the resort offers a range of amenities, including an indoor/outdoor pool, hot tub, fitness center, and a game room.

- **Family-Friendly:** With activities for kids, such as a playground and organized events, this is a great option for families traveling on a budget.

Cons:

- **Resort Fees:** Additional resort fees may apply, which can increase the overall cost of the stay.

- **Older Property:** Some areas of the resort may feel a bit dated, though it is generally well-maintained.

2. MOTEL 6 SOUTH LAKE TAHOE

Cost: Starting at $75 per night
Address: 2375 Lake Tahoe Blvd, South Lake Tahoe, CA 96150
Website: Motel 6 South Lake Tahoe

Pros:

- **Affordable Rates:** Motel 6 is known for offering some of the most affordable rates in the area, making it an excellent choice for budget-conscious travelers.

- **Central Location:** The motel is located along Lake Tahoe Boulevard, close to beaches, restaurants, and shopping, and a short drive to the Heavenly Gondola.

- **Pet-Friendly:** Motel 6 allows pets to stay free, which is a plus for travelers bringing their furry friends along.

- **No-Frills Comfort:** While basic, the rooms are clean and comfortable, offering good value for the price.

Cons:

- **Limited Amenities:** As a budget motel, amenities are minimal, with no on-site dining, fitness center, or pool.

- **Noise Levels:** The motel's location on a busy road means that noise can be an issue, particularly during peak tourist seasons.

3. BLUE JAY LODGE

Cost: Starting at $85 per night
Address: 4133 Cedar Ave, South Lake Tahoe, CA 96150
Website: Blue Jay Lodge

Pros:

- **Walkable Location:** Blue Jay Lodge is located just a short walk from the casinos at Stateline, the Heavenly Gondola, and the lake, making it easy to explore South Lake Tahoe without needing a car.

- **Affordable Rates:** The lodge offers budget-friendly rates without sacrificing comfort, making it a good option for travelers looking to save money.

- **Outdoor Pool:** During the warmer months, guests can enjoy the outdoor pool, a nice feature for a budget property.

- **Free Parking:** The lodge offers free parking, which is a bonus in an area where parking can be expensive.

Cons:

- **Basic Accommodations:** While clean and comfortable, the rooms are fairly basic, with dated decor and amenities.

- **No On-Site Dining:** There is no on-site restaurant, though there are several dining options within walking distance.

4. Tahoe City Inn

Cost: Starting at $90 per night
Address: 790 N Lake Blvd, Tahoe City, CA 96145
Website: Tahoe City Inn

Pros:

- **Central Tahoe City Location:** Located in the heart of Tahoe City, this inn is within walking distance of the lake, shops, and restaurants, as well as the Tahoe City Golf Course.

- **Comfortable Rooms:** The rooms are simple but offer comfortable beds, free Wi-Fi, and some even have fireplaces, adding a cozy touch.

- **Free Breakfast:** The inn provides a complimentary continental breakfast, helping you start your day without extra cost.

- **Affordable Rates:** Tahoe City Inn offers some of the most competitive rates in the Tahoe City area.

Cons:

- **No Pool or Fitness Center:** The inn lacks a pool or fitness facilities, which may be a downside for some travelers.

- **Older Property:** The inn is an older building, and while clean, some guests may find the decor and facilities a bit outdated.

5. 7 Seas Inn at Tahoe

Cost: Starting at $95 per night
Address: 4145 Manzanita Ave, South Lake Tahoe, CA 96150
Website: 7 Seas Inn at Tahoe

Pros:

- **Charming Atmosphere:** This boutique-style inn offers a cozy, welcoming atmosphere with rooms that are tastefully decorated and equipped with modern amenities.

- **Excellent Location:** Located within walking distance of the lake, Heavenly Gondola, and Stateline casinos, 7 Seas Inn is perfect for exploring South Lake Tahoe.

- **Complimentary Breakfast and Evening Reception:** Guests enjoy a complimentary hot breakfast and evening wine and cheese reception, adding value to the stay.

- **Personalized Service:** As a smaller property, the inn provides personalized service and a homey feel, which guests often appreciate.

Cons:

- **Small Property:** The inn is small, with limited common areas and no on-site pool or fitness center.

- **Limited Availability:** Due to its popularity and limited number of rooms, 7 Seas Inn can book up quickly, especially during peak times.

6. BIG PINES MOUNTAIN HOUSE

Cost: Starting at $80 per night
Address: 4083 Cedar Ave, South Lake Tahoe, CA 96150
Website: Big Pines Mountain House

Pros:

- **Affordable and Convenient:** Big Pines Mountain House offers budget-friendly accommodations with a great location, just a short walk from the lake, casinos, and Heavenly Gondola.

- **Pet-Friendly:** The hotel welcomes pets, making it a good choice for travelers with dogs.

- **Outdoor Pool:** Guests can enjoy the seasonal outdoor pool, which is a nice perk for a budget property.

- **Free Continental Breakfast:** A complimentary continental breakfast is provided, helping you save on meal costs.

Cons:

- **Basic Rooms:** The rooms are simple and functional, but some guests may find the decor and furnishings dated.

- **Noise Levels:** Given its central location and proximity to nightlife, noise can be an issue, particularly during weekends and holidays.

7. TAHOE VALLEY LODGE

Cost: Starting at $110 per night
Address: 2241 Lake Tahoe Blvd, South Lake Tahoe, CA 96150
Website: Tahoe Valley Lodge

Pros:

- **Charming Cabin-Style Rooms:** Tahoe Valley Lodge offers cabin-style rooms that are cozy and well-decorated, with wood paneling and rustic furnishings that reflect the mountain environment.

- **On-Site Spa:** Despite being a budget-friendly option, the lodge has an on-site spa offering a variety of treatments, adding extra value to your stay.

- **Proximity to Outdoor Activities:** The lodge is close to hiking and biking trails, as well as the lake, making it a convenient base for outdoor adventures.

- **Family-Friendly:** With larger rooms and kitchenettes available, the lodge is a good option for families looking for affordable accommodations.

Cons:

- **Older Property:** While charming, the lodge is an older property, and some areas may feel a bit worn.

- **Limited Dining Options:** There is no on-site restaurant, so guests will need to venture out for meals.

8. HOTEL BECKET

Cost: Starting at $100 per night
Address: 4003 Lake Tahoe Blvd, South Lake Tahoe, CA 96150
Website: Hotel Becket

Pros:

- **Central Location:** Hotel Becket is located right in the heart of South Lake Tahoe, close to the Heavenly Gondola, shopping, dining, and entertainment options.

- **Modern, Hip Atmosphere:** The hotel features a modern, boutique-style design with stylish rooms and contemporary decor, offering a more upscale feel at budget-friendly prices.

- **On-Site Dining:** Ten Crows BBQ, the hotel's on-site restaurant, offers delicious southern-style BBQ and is a convenient dining option.

- **Pet-Friendly:** Hotel Becket is pet-friendly, making it a great choice for travelers with pets.

Cons:

- **Resort Fees:** Additional resort fees may apply, which can increase the overall cost of the stay.

- **Limited Amenities:** The hotel offers fewer amenities compared to larger resorts, with no pool or fitness center on-site.

9.4 TIPS FOR BOOKING AND STAYING

Whether you're planning a budget-friendly trip, a luxurious getaway, or something in between, knowing a few insider tips can help you get the most out of your stay in Lake Tahoe. Here's a guide to making the most of your booking and staying experience in this beautiful destination.

1. BOOK EARLY FOR PEAK SEASONS

- **Timing is Everything:** Lake Tahoe is a year-round destination, with peak seasons during the winter for skiing and the summer for beach and hiking activities. Booking your accommodation early—ideally several months in advance—can secure better rates and a wider selection of places to stay.

- **Holiday Weekends:** If your trip coincides with major holidays (e.g., Christmas, New Year's, Fourth of July), it's crucial to book even earlier as accommodations fill up quickly and prices can soar.

2. CONSIDER OFF-PEAK TRAVEL

- **Shoulder Seasons:** Visiting during the shoulder seasons—late spring (April to June) and early fall (September to October)—can provide the best of both worlds: pleasant weather, fewer crowds, and lower prices.

- **Midweek Stays:** If your schedule allows, consider booking your stay from Sunday to Thursday. Midweek rates are often lower, and popular attractions are less crowded.

3. Use Price Comparison Tools

- **Online Booking Sites:** Use websites like Booking.com, Expedia, or Kayak to compare prices across different hotels and lodges. Sometimes, booking directly through the hotel's website can also offer perks like free breakfast or waived resort fees.

- **Flexible Dates:** If your travel dates are flexible, use price comparison tools to see if shifting your stay by a day or two could result in significant savings.

4. Look for Package Deals

- **Bundled Savings:** Many resorts and hotels in Lake Tahoe offer package deals that include lift tickets, spa treatments, or dining credits. These packages can provide substantial savings, especially if you plan to take advantage of these services.

- **Group Discounts:** If you're traveling with a group, look for group discounts or consider booking a larger vacation rental or condo, which can be more cost-effective than multiple hotel rooms.

5. Consider Location Carefully

- **Proximity to Activities:** Choose your accommodation based on the activities you plan to enjoy. If skiing is your main focus, staying at a ski-in/ski-out resort like The Ritz-Carlton, Lake Tahoe, or a nearby lodge in Northstar or Heavenly will save time and effort. For summer activities, a lakeside hotel or cabin in Tahoe City or South Lake Tahoe might be ideal.

- **Transportation Needs:** If you plan to explore different parts of Lake Tahoe, consider staying somewhere centrally located like South Lake Tahoe or Incline Village. Also, think about parking availability and public transportation options if you don't want to drive everywhere.

6. Read Reviews and Check Amenities

- **User Reviews:** Before booking, read recent reviews on sites like TripAdvisor or Google to get a sense of what other travelers experienced. Pay attention to comments about cleanliness, service, and amenities.

- **Essential Amenities:** Make sure the accommodation offers amenities that are important to you, such as free Wi-Fi, parking, a kitchenette, or pet-friendly rooms if you're traveling with pets.

7. Take Advantage of Loyalty Programs

- **Hotel Loyalty Programs:** If you're a member of a hotel loyalty program (e.g., Marriott Bonvoy, Hilton Honors), check if there are properties in Lake Tahoe where you can earn or redeem points for your stay.

- **Credit Card Rewards:** Some travel credit cards offer points or cashback when booking through their portals, or additional perks like room upgrades and late check-out.

8. Be Aware of Additional Fees

- **Resort Fees:** Many Lake Tahoe resorts charge daily resort fees that cover amenities like Wi-Fi, parking, or use of the pool and fitness center. Make sure to factor these into your budget.

- **Cancellation Policies:** Check the cancellation policy before booking. Non-refundable rates are often cheaper but may not be worth the savings if your plans change.

9. Pack for the Season

- **Winter Gear:** If visiting in winter, pack appropriately for snow conditions. Layers, waterproof clothing, and sturdy snow boots are essential. If you're skiing or snowboarding, you might want to bring your own gear or check in advance for rental options at your accommodation.

- **Summer Essentials:** In the summer, pack sunscreen, hats, and swimwear. Don't forget hiking boots if you plan to explore the trails. Even in summer, evenings can be cool, so bring a light jacket or sweater.

10. PLAN FOR MEALS

- **Dining Options:** Consider the availability of dining options near your accommodation. If you're staying in a cabin or a property with a kitchenette, plan to cook some meals to save money. Many grocery stores and markets around Lake Tahoe offer fresh, local produce.

- **Reservations:** For popular restaurants, especially during peak seasons, make reservations in advance to avoid long waits.

11. ENJOY THE FREE ACTIVITIES

- **Outdoor Recreation:** Lake Tahoe offers a wealth of free outdoor activities, from hiking and biking to beach days and stargazing. Many trails, parks, and public beaches are free to access, offering beautiful views without breaking the bank.

- **Local Events:** Check out local events like farmers' markets, outdoor concerts, or festivals, which often provide free entertainment and a chance to experience Tahoe's local culture.

12. RESPECT THE ENVIRONMENT

- **Leave No Trace:** Lake Tahoe's natural beauty is one of its biggest draws, and it's essential to keep it that way. Follow Leave No Trace principles—dispose of waste properly, respect wildlife, and minimize your impact on the environment.

- **Sustainability Practices:** Support accommodations and businesses that prioritize sustainability. Many properties in Tahoe are committed to eco-friendly practices like energy conservation, water-saving initiatives, and recycling programs.

CHAPTER 10: ITINERARY PLANNING
10.1 CRAFTING THE PERFECT ITINERARY

1. DETERMINE THE LENGTH OF YOUR STAY

Before diving into the details, start by defining how many days you'll be spending in Lake Tahoe. This will help you prioritize activities and allocate time appropriately.

- **Weekend Getaway (2-3 Days):** Focus on the must-see attractions and activities. Plan for one major activity per day, such as skiing, hiking, or a scenic drive around the lake.

- **Extended Stay (4-7 Days):** With more time, you can explore a wider range of activities, including multiple outdoor adventures, cultural experiences, and relaxation time.

- **Longer Vacations (8+ Days):** For those with ample time, consider a mix of leisurely exploration, day trips to nearby attractions, and time to immerse yourself in Lake Tahoe's natural beauty.

2. PRIORITIZE YOUR MUST-DO ACTIVITIES

Lake Tahoe offers a diverse range of activities year-round, so it's important to identify your must-do experiences early on. Consider the season and your personal interests when planning your itinerary.

- **Winter Activities:**

  - **Skiing and Snowboarding:** If visiting in winter, skiing or snowboarding at one of Tahoe's premier resorts like Heavenly, Northstar, or Squaw Valley should be at the top of your list.

  - **Snowshoeing and Cross-Country Skiing:** For a quieter winter experience, explore Tahoe's scenic trails on snowshoes or cross-country skis. Popular spots include Spooner Lake and Tahoe Meadows.

  - **Snowmobiling:** Thrill-seekers can enjoy guided snowmobile tours through Tahoe's backcountry, offering stunning views and an adrenaline rush.

- **Summer Activities:**

  - **Hiking:** Lake Tahoe is a hiker's paradise, with trails ranging from easy walks to challenging climbs. Don't miss the Eagle Lake Trail or the more strenuous Mount Tallac hike for breathtaking views.

  - **Water Sports:** Kayaking, paddleboarding, and swimming are popular summer activities. Rent equipment at spots like Sand Harbor or Emerald Bay for a day on the water.

  - **Biking:** Explore the region on two wheels, with options like the scenic Tahoe Rim Trail or the paved Truckee River Bike Path.

- **Year-Round Activities:**

  - **Scenic Drives:** The 72-mile drive around Lake Tahoe offers some of the most spectacular views in the area. Plan stops at viewpoints like Inspiration Point and Logan Shoals.

- Gambling and Entertainment: If you're staying in South Lake Tahoe, visit the Stateline casinos for some evening entertainment, dining, and shows.

- Spa and Wellness: Schedule time for relaxation at one of the area's luxury spas, such as The Ritz-Carlton Spa or Spa Edgewood.

3. MAP OUT YOUR DAYS

Once you've identified your must-do activities, it's time to map out your days. Consider the location of each activity to minimize travel time and maximize your experience.

- **Day 1: Arrival and Acclimatization**

  - **Morning:** Arrive in Lake Tahoe, check into your accommodation, and get settled.

  - **Afternoon:** Take a leisurely stroll along the lake, perhaps visiting Tahoe City or South Lake Tahoe for some light exploration.

  - **Evening:** Enjoy dinner at a local restaurant. If staying in South Lake Tahoe, consider dining at Edgewood Restaurant or The Lake House.

- **Day 2: Adventure and Exploration**

  - **Morning:** Start your day with a hearty breakfast before heading to a major activity like skiing, hiking, or kayaking.

  - **Afternoon:** Continue your outdoor adventure. If skiing, take advantage of the slopes. If hiking, pack a lunch and enjoy a scenic picnic.

- o **Evening:** Unwind with a relaxing evening. Consider a sunset cruise on the lake or visit a local brewery or wine bar.

- **Day 3: Scenic Drives and Cultural Experiences**

  - o **Morning:** Drive around the lake, stopping at key viewpoints like Emerald Bay, Sand Harbor, and Donner Summit.

  - o **Afternoon:** Visit a local museum or gallery, such as the Tahoe Maritime Museum or the Gatekeeper's Museum in Tahoe City.

  - o **Evening:** Enjoy a final dinner at a local favorite, reflecting on the day's experiences.

- **Day 4+: Extending Your Stay**

  - o **Days 4-7:** Use additional days to explore more trails, take day trips to nearby attractions like Truckee or Carson City, or simply relax by the lake.

  - o **Days 8+:** If staying longer, mix in some leisure time with new activities. Consider exploring the less-visited areas of Tahoe, such as the West Shore or the Nevada side of the lake.

4. INCORPORATE DOWNTIME AND FLEXIBILITY

While it's tempting to pack your itinerary with activities, don't forget to include downtime. Relaxing by the lake, enjoying a spa day, or simply taking a leisurely walk can make your trip more enjoyable.

- **Afternoon Breaks:** Plan for some free time each afternoon to relax, explore at your own pace, or discover hidden gems you might have missed in your initial planning.

- **Flexible Days:** Leave one or two days unplanned to allow for spontaneous adventures or to revisit a favorite spot.

5. PLAN FOR MEALS AND DINING EXPERIENCES

Dining is an essential part of any trip, and Lake Tahoe offers a range of options from casual eateries to fine dining.

- **Breakfast:** Start your day with a hearty breakfast. Consider local favorites like Fire Sign Café in Tahoe City or Driftwood Café in South Lake Tahoe.

- **Lunch:** Pack a picnic if you're hiking or enjoy a lakeside meal at one of the many casual dining spots.

- **Dinner:** For a special evening, book a table at one of Tahoe's fine dining restaurants, such as the Lone Eagle Grille in Incline Village or Evan's American Gourmet Café in South Lake Tahoe.

6. PREPARE FOR THE WEATHER AND ALTITUDE

Lake Tahoe's weather can change quickly, and the altitude can affect visitors differently, so it's important to prepare.

- **Weather:** Check the weather forecast before your trip and pack layers, as temperatures can vary significantly throughout the day. In winter, ensure you have appropriate snow gear.

- **Altitude:** Lake Tahoe sits at an elevation of over 6,000 feet. To avoid altitude sickness, stay hydrated, avoid alcohol on your first day, and take it easy on physical activities until you're acclimated.

7. CONSIDER TRANSPORTATION OPTIONS

Getting around Lake Tahoe can be part of the adventure, but it's important to plan how you'll travel between activities.

- **Car Rentals:** Renting a car is often the best option, especially if you plan to explore multiple areas around the lake. Ensure your rental car is equipped for winter driving if you're visiting in the snowy season.

- **Public Transportation:** The Tahoe Transportation District offers bus services around the lake, which can be a convenient and eco-friendly option.

- **Biking:** In the warmer months, consider renting a bike for short trips or to explore the local trails.

8. MAKE RESERVATIONS AND BOOK ACTIVITIES IN ADVANCE

To avoid disappointment, make reservations for popular activities, dining, and accommodations in advance, especially during peak seasons.

- **Dining:** Book dinner reservations at popular restaurants well ahead of your trip.

- **Activities:** For ski rentals, guided tours, or boat rentals, book in advance to secure your spot.

- **Accommodations:** Ensure your lodging is booked well in advance, particularly if you're visiting during a busy holiday weekend or a major event.

9. STAY INFORMED AND FLEXIBLE

Finally, stay informed about local events, weather changes, and any travel advisories that might affect your trip.

- **Local Events:** Check local event calendars for festivals, concerts, or special activities that might be happening during your stay.

- **Weather Alerts:** Keep an eye on weather updates, especially in winter, to avoid being caught off guard by sudden snowstorms or road closures.

- **Flexibility:** Even with the best planning, things can change. Be flexible and ready to adjust your itinerary if needed.

10.2 BEST TIME OF YEAR TO VISIT

Lake Tahoe is a year-round destination, offering something special in every season. The best time to visit depends on the type of activities you want to enjoy, your tolerance for crowds, and your budget. Here's a detailed guide to help you decide when to plan your trip to Lake Tahoe.

WINTER (DECEMBER TO FEBRUARY): A SNOW LOVER'S PARADISE

Why Visit in Winter:

- **Skiing and Snowboarding:** Winter is prime time for snow sports enthusiasts. Lake Tahoe is home to some of the best ski resorts in the country, including Heavenly, Northstar, and Squaw Valley (now Palisades Tahoe). With deep powder, extensive trails, and stunning alpine scenery, it's a skier's dream.

- **Snowshoeing and Cross-Country Skiing:** For those who prefer a quieter winter experience, the snow-covered trails around Lake Tahoe offer excellent opportunities for snowshoeing and cross-country skiing.

- **Holiday Festivities:** The winter season brings a festive atmosphere to the region, with holiday lights, special events, and a variety of winter activities for families.

Considerations:

- **Crowds:** The holiday season, particularly around Christmas and New Year's, is one of the busiest times of the year. Ski resorts and accommodations can be crowded, and prices are at their peak.

- **Weather:** Winter storms can bring heavy snowfall, which is great for skiing but can make travel difficult. Be prepared for winter driving conditions and potential road closures.

Best For:

- Snow sports enthusiasts, families looking for a festive winter getaway, and anyone who loves the magic of a snowy landscape.

SPRING (MARCH TO MAY): A TIME OF TRANSITION

Why Visit in Spring:

- **Spring Skiing:** Early spring still offers good skiing conditions, especially in March. As the season progresses, you can enjoy sunny days on the slopes with fewer crowds.

- **Wildflower Blooms:** By late April and May, the snow begins to melt, revealing vibrant wildflowers and lush greenery in the lower elevations. This is a great time for hiking and nature walks.

- **Lower Prices:** Spring is considered a shoulder season, meaning you can often find better deals on accommodations and activities as the winter crowds disperse and before the summer rush begins.

Considerations:

- **Variable Weather:** Spring weather in Tahoe can be unpredictable. You might experience a mix of lingering snow, rain, and sunny days. Some trails and roads may still be inaccessible due to snow.

- **Limited Activities:** Some activities, like boating and certain high-elevation hikes, may not be fully available until late spring.

Best For:

- Budget-conscious travelers, spring skiers, and those looking to experience Tahoe's natural beauty without the crowds.

Summer (June to August): The Season of Sun and Fun

Why Visit in Summer:

- **Outdoor Recreation:** Summer is the best time for enjoying Lake Tahoe's extensive outdoor activities. From hiking, mountain biking, and camping to kayaking, paddleboarding, and swimming, the options are endless.

- **Perfect Weather:** With warm, sunny days and cool nights, summer weather in Tahoe is ideal for outdoor adventures. Daytime highs typically range from the 70s to low 80s (Fahrenheit), perfect for exploring the region's trails and beaches.

- **Festivals and Events:** Summer is festival season in Tahoe, with a variety of outdoor concerts, art festivals, and community events. Highlights include the Lake Tahoe Shakespeare Festival and the American Century Championship celebrity golf tournament.

Considerations:

- **Crowds:** Summer is peak tourist season in Tahoe, especially in July and August. Expect busy beaches, full campgrounds, and higher prices for accommodations.

- **Wildfire Risk:** Late summer can bring an increased risk of wildfires in the region, which may affect air quality and outdoor activities.

Best For:

- Outdoor enthusiasts, families, and anyone looking to soak up the sun and enjoy Tahoe's natural beauty at its fullest.

Fall (September to November): A Peaceful Retreat

Why Visit in Fall:

- **Spectacular Fall Foliage:** Autumn brings stunning fall colors to Tahoe, with aspen trees turning vibrant shades of yellow and orange. The fall foliage typically peaks in late September and early October.

- **Mild Weather:** Early fall offers mild, comfortable weather, perfect for hiking, biking, and enjoying the outdoors without the summer crowds.

- **Tranquility:** Fall is one of the quietest times of the year in Tahoe, making it an ideal season for a peaceful retreat. Accommodations are more affordable, and the trails and beaches are less crowded.

Considerations:

- **Cooler Temperatures:** As fall progresses, temperatures drop, especially at night. While the days can be pleasantly warm, evenings and mornings can be quite chilly.

- **Limited Activities:** Some seasonal businesses and activities start to wind down after Labor Day, and certain facilities may have reduced hours or close for the season.

Best For:

- Couples looking for a romantic getaway, photographers and nature lovers, and anyone seeking a quieter, more serene Tahoe experience.

10.3 Seasonal Activities and Events

Whether you're drawn to the snowy slopes in winter, the vibrant festivals in summer, or the tranquil beauty of fall, there's always something happening in this picturesque region. Here's a guide to the seasonal activities and events that make Lake Tahoe a year-round hotspot for visitors.

WINTER (DECEMBER TO FEBRUARY): EMBRACE THE SNOWY WONDERLAND

Activities:

1. **Skiing and Snowboarding:**

     o **Top Resorts:** Heavenly Mountain Resort, Northstar California Resort, Palisades Tahoe (formerly Squaw Valley).

     o **Details:** These world-class resorts offer slopes for all skill levels, from beginner to expert, along with terrain parks, ski schools, and après-ski activities.

2. **Snowshoeing and Cross-Country Skiing:**

     o **Best Spots:** Spooner Lake, Tahoe Meadows, and Camp Richardson.

     o **Details:** Enjoy peaceful, snowy trails with stunning views of the lake and surrounding mountains.

3. **Ice Skating:**

     o **Locations:** Heavenly Village Ice Rink (South Lake Tahoe), Northstar Village Rink (Truckee).

     o **Details:** Ice skating is a family-friendly activity perfect for an afternoon of fun. The rinks often have fire pits and hot cocoa stands nearby.

4. **Snowmobiling:**

- o **Tours Available:** Zephyr Cove Resort, Lake Tahoe Adventures.

- o **Details:** Explore Tahoe's backcountry on a guided snowmobile tour, which offers both thrilling speed and incredible vistas.

Events:

1. **SnowGlobe Music Festival (Late December):**

   - o **Location:** South Lake Tahoe.

   - o **Details:** This three-day outdoor festival features top electronic, hip-hop, and indie music acts, set against the snowy backdrop of Tahoe's mountains.

2. **Heavenly Holidays (December):**

   - o **Location:** Heavenly Village, South Lake Tahoe.

   - o **Details:** A month-long celebration featuring holiday lights, ice skating, concerts, and a festive atmosphere. The event culminates with a New Year's Eve celebration.

3. **WinterWonderGrass Tahoe (March):**

   - o **Location:** Palisades Tahoe.

   - o **Details:** A bluegrass and roots music festival combined with craft beer tastings, all set in a stunning mountain setting.

SPRING (MARCH TO MAY): A TIME OF RENEWAL

Activities:

1. **Spring Skiing:**

- Best Time: March and early April.

- Details: Enjoy skiing with softer snow, longer days, and plenty of sunshine. Many resorts offer discounted lift tickets during spring.

2. **Wildflower Hikes:**

- Popular Trails: Cascade Falls, Eagle Lake, and Mount Tallac (lower elevations).

- Details: As the snow melts, wildflowers begin to bloom, creating colorful landscapes perfect for hiking and photography.

3. **Fishing:**

- Best Spots: Truckee River, Lake Tahoe shoreline, Fallen Leaf Lake.

- Details: Spring is a great time for fishing as the waters are cooler and fish are more active. Both shore and boat fishing are popular.

4. **Golfing:**

- Top Courses: Edgewood Tahoe Golf Course, Incline Village Championship Course.

- Details: Golf season begins in late spring, offering stunning views and challenging courses.

Events:

1. **Made in Tahoe Festival (May):**

- Location: Palisades Tahoe.

- **Details:** This annual festival celebrates local art, culture, and goods with over 100 vendors, live music, and performances.

2. **Earth Day Celebrations (April):**

   - **Locations:** Various locations around Lake Tahoe, including Incline Village and South Lake Tahoe.

   - **Details:** Earth Day events feature eco-friendly vendors, educational exhibits, live music, and activities for all ages, promoting environmental stewardship.

3. **Tahoe Film Fest (Late April):**

   - **Location:** North Lake Tahoe.

   - **Details:** This film festival showcases independent films, environmental documentaries, and Latin American cinema, with a focus on raising awareness about environmental issues.

SUMMER (JUNE TO AUGUST): THE SEASON OF SUN AND FUN

Activities:

1. **Hiking and Mountain Biking:**

   - **Top Trails:** Tahoe Rim Trail, Eagle Rock Trail, Desolation Wilderness.

   - **Details:** Summer is the perfect time for exploring Tahoe's extensive network of trails, offering everything from easy walks to challenging backcountry adventures.

2. **Water Sports:**

   - **Activities:** Kayaking, paddleboarding, swimming, jet skiing, and boating.

- Best Locations: Sand Harbor, Emerald Bay, Kings Beach.

- Details: The crystal-clear waters of Lake Tahoe are perfect for all types of water activities. Rentals are available at most beaches.

3. Camping:

- Popular Campgrounds: D.L. Bliss State Park, Fallen Leaf Campground, Meeks Bay Resort.

- Details: Enjoy stargazing, campfires, and the tranquility of nature at one of Tahoe's many campgrounds.

4. Golfing:

- Top Courses: Edgewood Tahoe Golf Course, Old Brockway Golf Course.

- Details: Enjoy a round of golf with panoramic views of the lake and mountains.

Events:

1. Lake Tahoe Shakespeare Festival (July-August):

- Location: Sand Harbor, Incline Village.

- Details: Experience world-class Shakespearean performances in a stunning outdoor amphitheater with the lake as a backdrop.

2. American Century Championship (July):

- Location: Edgewood Tahoe Golf Course, South Lake Tahoe.

- Details: This celebrity golf tournament draws stars from sports and entertainment, offering spectators the chance to see their favorite celebrities up close.

3. **Live at Lakeview Summer Music Series (June-August):**

   o **Location:** Lakeview Commons, South Lake Tahoe.

   o **Details:** A free weekly concert series featuring local and regional bands, food vendors, and a beer garden, all set against the beautiful backdrop of Lake Tahoe.

4. **Tahoe Rim Trail Endurance Runs (July):**

   o **Location:** Various trails around Lake Tahoe.

   o **Details:** These ultra-marathon races challenge participants to traverse some of the most scenic and rugged trails in the region.

FALL (SEPTEMBER TO NOVEMBER): A SEASON OF TRANQUILITY

Activities:

1. **Fall Foliage Hikes:**

   o **Best Spots:** Hope Valley, Marlette Lake, Spooner Lake.

   o **Details:** Fall colors peak in late September and early October, offering breathtaking views of golden aspens and crimson maples against the backdrop of blue skies and mountains.

2. **Fishing:**

   o **Best Locations:** Truckee River, Lake Tahoe, Donner Lake.

   o **Details:** Fall is an excellent time for fishing, with cooler waters and less competition from other anglers.

3. **Scenic Drives:**

- o **Top Routes:** The 72-mile drive around Lake Tahoe, Hope Valley, and Monitor Pass.

- o **Details:** Take a leisurely drive to enjoy the fall colors and scenic vistas that Lake Tahoe has to offer.

4. **Mountain Biking:**

- o **Popular Trails:** Flume Trail, Tahoe Rim Trail, Mr. Toad's Wild Ride.

- o **Details:** Cooler temperatures make fall an ideal time for mountain biking, with trails offering everything from beginner to advanced challenges.

Events:

1. **Oktoberfest (September-October):**

- o **Locations:** Camp Richardson (South Lake Tahoe), Squaw Valley.

- o **Details:** These family-friendly events celebrate Bavarian culture with beer, bratwurst, live music, and games. The Camp Richardson Oktoberfest is particularly popular for its laid-back atmosphere.

2. **Tahoe City Harvest Festival (October):**

- o **Location:** Tahoe City.

- o **Details:** A community-focused event featuring a pumpkin patch, hayrides, live music, and local crafts, perfect for families.

3. **Fall AleFest & Chicken Wing Cook-Off (September):**

- o **Location:** MontBleu Resort Casino & Spa, South Lake Tahoe.

- ○ **Details:** This annual event combines craft beer tastings with a chicken wing cook-off, where local chefs compete for the title of best wings in Tahoe.

10.4 RESOURCES FOR PLANNING

1. OFFICIAL TOURISM WEBSITES

Visit Lake Tahoe

- **Website:** Visit Lake Tahoe

- **Details:** This official tourism website for Lake Tahoe offers comprehensive information on things to do, places to stay, and upcoming events. It's a great starting point for planning your trip.

Tahoe South

- **Website:** Tahoe South

- **Details:** Focused on the South Lake Tahoe area, this site provides detailed information on lodging, dining, and activities specific to the southern region of the lake. It also features a useful event calendar.

North Lake Tahoe

- **Website:** Go Tahoe North

- **Details:** For those exploring the northern part of Lake Tahoe, this website offers insights into local events, outdoor activities, and travel tips. It's especially helpful for finding information on North Shore communities like Tahoe City, Kings Beach, and Incline Village.

2. ACCOMMODATION BOOKING PLATFORMS

Booking.com

- **Website:** Booking.com

- **Details:** A popular platform for booking hotels, motels, resorts, and vacation rentals. It offers a wide range of filters to help you find the perfect accommodation, whether you're looking for luxury or budget-friendly options.

Airbnb

- **Website:** Airbnb

- **Details:** Airbnb offers a variety of unique accommodations, from cozy cabins to lakeside villas. It's an excellent resource for finding places that offer a more personalized experience, often with the chance to interact with local hosts.

VRBO

- **Website:** VRBO

- **Details:** Similar to Airbnb, VRBO focuses on vacation rentals, including homes, condos, and cabins. It's ideal for families or groups looking for spacious accommodations.

3. WEATHER AND ROAD CONDITIONS

National Weather Service – Lake Tahoe

- **Website:** NWS Lake Tahoe

- **Details:** Get up-to-date weather forecasts specific to the Lake Tahoe region. This site is crucial for planning outdoor activities and preparing for changing conditions, especially in winter.

Caltrans Road Conditions

- **Website:** Caltrans QuickMap
- **Details:** For those driving to or around Lake Tahoe, this tool provides real-time road conditions, including closures, traffic, and chain control requirements during winter.

Nevada Department of Transportation

- **Website:** NDOT
- **Details:** This site offers road condition updates and travel alerts for the Nevada side of Lake Tahoe, including routes leading to Incline Village and Stateline.

4. OUTDOOR RECREATION AND TRAIL INFORMATION

AllTrails

- **Website:** AllTrails
- **Details:** AllTrails is an excellent resource for finding detailed information on hiking, biking, and snowshoeing trails in Lake Tahoe. You can search by difficulty, distance, and user reviews, and even download maps for offline use.

Tahoe Rim Trail Association

- **Website:** Tahoe Rim Trail Association
- **Details:** The official site for the Tahoe Rim Trail provides maps, trail conditions, and detailed guides for hiking, biking, and backpacking the 165-mile trail that encircles Lake Tahoe.

U.S. Forest Service – Lake Tahoe Basin Management Unit

- **Website:** USFS Lake Tahoe

- **Details:** This site offers comprehensive information on recreation areas, campgrounds, and wilderness permits in the Lake Tahoe Basin. It's a valuable resource for those planning to explore the more remote areas of the region.

5. EVENT AND ACTIVITY PLANNING

Lake Tahoe Events Calendar

- **Website:** Tahoe Events Calendar

- **Details:** Tahoetopia offers an extensive calendar of events happening around Lake Tahoe, including concerts, festivals, outdoor activities, and more. It's a great way to find out what's happening during your visit.

Eventbrite

- **Website:** Eventbrite Lake Tahoe

- **Details:** Eventbrite lists local events, workshops, and activities in Lake Tahoe. It's particularly useful for finding smaller, niche events or activities that might not be widely advertised.

6. DINING AND LOCAL CUISINE

Yelp

- **Website:** Yelp Lake Tahoe

- **Details:** Yelp provides user reviews, photos, and ratings for restaurants, cafes, and bars in Lake Tahoe. It's a handy tool for finding top-rated dining spots and hidden gems.

OpenTable

- **Website:** OpenTable

- **Details:** OpenTable allows you to make reservations at many of Lake Tahoe's restaurants. It's particularly useful for securing a table at popular dining spots during peak seasons.

7. TRAVEL GUIDES AND BLOGS

KIM MIA – Lake Tahoe

- **Details:** LIM MIA offers a comprehensive travel guide to Lake Tahoe, including tips on where to stay, eat, and play. It's a reliable resource for first-time visitors.

Lake Tahoe Travel Blog

- **Website:** Lake Tahoe Travel Blog
- **Details:** This blog offers insider tips, trip ideas, and detailed posts about activities, events, and hidden spots in Lake Tahoe. It's a great resource for finding unique experiences and off-the-beaten-path adventures.

TripAdvisor Lake Tahoe

- **Website:** TripAdvisor Lake Tahoe
- **Details:** TripAdvisor provides a wealth of user-generated reviews and travel tips for Lake Tahoe. It covers everything from accommodations and restaurants to tours and attractions.

8. TRANSPORTATION

South Tahoe Airporter

- **Website:** South Tahoe Airporter

- **Details:** This shuttle service offers transportation between Reno-Tahoe International Airport and South Lake Tahoe. It's a convenient option if you're flying into the area.

Tahoe Transportation District

- **Website:** Tahoe Transportation District

- **Details:** The TTD provides public bus services around Lake Tahoe, including routes to major towns, resorts, and attractions. It's a useful option for getting around without a car.

Uber and Lyft

- **Apps Available:** Uber and Lyft are widely available in the Lake Tahoe area, providing a convenient way to get around, especially for short trips or evenings out.

9. SUSTAINABILITY AND ENVIRONMENTAL STEWARDSHIP

Keep Tahoe Blue

- **Website:** Keep Tahoe Blue

- **Details:** This organization is dedicated to protecting Lake Tahoe's environment. Their website offers tips on how visitors can help preserve the lake's clarity and natural beauty, including responsible travel practices and volunteer opportunities.

Leave No Trace Center for Outdoor Ethics

- **Website:** Leave No Trace

- **Details:** Learn about Leave No Trace principles to minimize your impact on the environment while exploring Lake Tahoe. This resource is especially important for those planning outdoor activities in sensitive areas.

CONCLUSION

As you wrap up your journey through this comprehensive Lake Tahoe Travel Guide 2025, it's clear that this enchanting destination offers something truly extraordinary for every traveler. Whether you're drawn to the pristine waters, the towering pine trees, or the majestic mountain peaks, Lake Tahoe's natural beauty captivates the soul and leaves an indelible mark on all who visit.

A YEAR-ROUND DESTINATION OF ENDLESS POSSIBILITIES

Lake Tahoe is a destination that defies seasonal boundaries. It's a place where every season brings its own unique charm and opportunities for adventure. In the winter, the region transforms into a snowy wonderland, attracting skiers, snowboarders, and those who simply wish to experience the serene beauty of snow-covered landscapes. The winter months are also a time of festive celebrations, with holiday events, music festivals, and cozy evenings by the fire that make this season truly special.

Spring in Lake Tahoe is a time of renewal, when the snow begins to melt, and the first signs of life return to the mountains and valleys. It's a season that offers the best of both worlds—spring skiing on sun-drenched slopes and the budding of wildflowers in the meadows below. As the days grow longer, the promise of summer begins to fill the air, bringing with it a sense of excitement and anticipation.

Summer is when Lake Tahoe truly shines. The crystal-clear waters of the lake beckon swimmers, kayakers, and paddleboarders, while the surrounding mountains offer endless opportunities for hiking, mountain biking, and camping. The vibrant summer sun illuminates the region's stunning landscapes, making every outdoor adventure feel like a once-in-a-lifetime experience. The warm days are balanced by cool, refreshing nights, perfect for stargazing or enjoying a lakeside campfire.

As summer fades, fall emerges with a quieter, more reflective beauty. The golden hues of aspen trees and the crisp, cool air create an atmosphere of tranquility that is perfect for those seeking a peaceful retreat. Fall is a time to slow down, take in the beauty of the changing seasons, and enjoy the serenity of Lake Tahoe without the summer crowds.

A PLACE OF RICH HISTORY AND CULTURE

Beyond its natural beauty, Lake Tahoe is a region steeped in history and culture. The Washoe Tribe, the original inhabitants of the Lake Tahoe Basin, have a deep spiritual connection to the land, and their cultural heritage is still very much alive today. Visitors can learn about the Washoe people's history and traditions through various cultural experiences, museums, and educational programs that are available throughout the area.

The region's history is also marked by the Gold Rush and the development of the Western frontier, with many historic sites and towns offering a glimpse into the past. From the charming streets of Truckee to the grand estates of the West Shore, Lake Tahoe's history is preserved in its architecture, museums, and cultural landmarks.

ADVENTURES FOR EVERY TYPE OF TRAVELER

Whether you're an adrenaline junkie looking for your next big adventure or a traveler seeking rest and relaxation, Lake Tahoe has something for everyone. The outdoor enthusiast will find no shortage of activities, from skiing and snowboarding in the winter to hiking, biking, and water sports in the summer. For those who prefer a more leisurely pace, the region offers scenic drives, peaceful beaches, and luxurious spas where you can unwind and rejuvenate.

Families will find Lake Tahoe to be an ideal destination, with a wide range of family-friendly activities and events that cater to all ages. From interactive nature walks and educational programs to festivals and outdoor concerts, there's always something to keep both kids and adults entertained.

Couples will discover a romantic side of Lake Tahoe, with cozy cabins, intimate dining experiences, and breathtaking views that set the perfect backdrop for a memorable getaway. Whether it's a quiet hike to a secluded spot or a sunset cruise on the lake, the region's natural beauty creates an atmosphere of romance and connection.

SUSTAINABILITY AND STEWARDSHIP: PROTECTING THE JEWEL OF THE SIERRA

As visitors to this incredible region, it's important to recognize the role we all play in preserving Lake Tahoe's pristine environment for future generations. The lake's famed clarity and the surrounding wilderness are delicate ecosystems that require thoughtful stewardship. By practicing Leave No Trace principles, supporting local conservation efforts, and choosing sustainable travel options, we can all contribute to keeping Lake Tahoe beautiful.

Local organizations like Keep Tahoe Blue are dedicated to protecting the lake and its environment, offering volunteer opportunities and educational programs that visitors can participate in. Supporting businesses that prioritize sustainability and environmental responsibility is another way to ensure that Lake Tahoe remains a vibrant and healthy destination for years to come.

YOUR JOURNEY DOESN'T END HERE

As you prepare to leave Lake Tahoe, remember that your journey doesn't have to end. The memories you've created—the first sight of the lake's shimmering waters, the thrill of conquering a mountain trail, the quiet moments spent watching the sun set over the Sierra—will stay with you long after you've returned home.

Lake Tahoe has a way of calling people back, time and time again. Whether it's the allure of a new season, the discovery of a hidden gem you missed on your first visit, or the simple desire to reconnect with nature, there's always a reason to return.

As you reflect on your time here, take with you not only the experiences you've had but also a sense of connection to this remarkable place. Lake Tahoe is more than just a destination—it's a reminder of the beauty and wonder of the natural world, a place where the mountains meet the sky, and where every moment is an opportunity to be inspired.

Lake Tahoe is a place that transcends the ordinary. It's a destination that offers adventure, relaxation, culture, and natural beauty in equal measure. As you close this chapter of your travels, know that you've experienced something truly special—a place where the beauty of nature and the warmth of community come together to create memories that will last a lifetime.

So, whether you're already planning your next trip or simply taking a moment to savor the experiences you've had, remember that Lake Tahoe will always be here, ready to welcome you back with open arms and endless possibilities. Until next time, safe travels, and keep the spirit of Lake Tahoe alive in your heart.

Made in the USA
Las Vegas, NV
12 December 2024

13890095R00118